ZEN
is for Everyone

"In chopping wood and carrying water, Therein lies the wonderful Dao."
*Hui Yuan, 6th Zen Patriarch (*Liang kai, early 13th century).

Opposite: Zen Master Liang kai (Sung Dynasty, 960–1281)

ZEN is for Everyone

Translated and Adapted for Practical Use
by Michael Saso

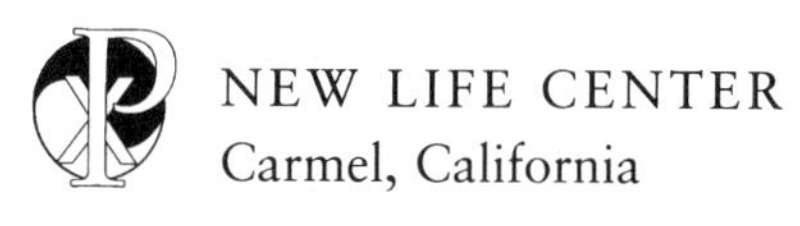
NEW LIFE CENTER
Carmel, California

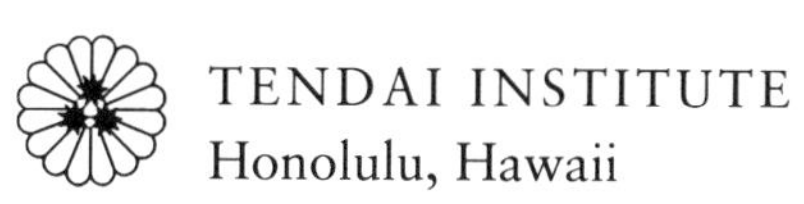
TENDAI INSTITUTE
Honolulu, Hawaii

ISBN 1-929431-02-3

Camera ready copy was prepared by the author

This book was printed on acid free paper, and meets the guidelines for permanence and durability of the Council on Library Resources

Sponsors: Tendai Foundation, New York, NY
New Life Center, Carmel, CA.

Distributed by
University of Hawai'i Press
2840 Kolowalu Street
Honolulu, Hawai'i 96822

TABLE OF CONTENTS

*****

FOREWORD

The *Xiao Jhiguan* (Jpn: *Shoshikan*, Little Manual of Samatha-Vipasyana Meditation) is a beginner's guide to Zen (Chan) practice. It teaches anyone who picks up and reads its straightforward message, how to do Zen meditation. Zen practice bears fruit when these simple rules are followed. The manual is attributed to Zhi Yi (Chih I, 538-597), the fourth master of Tientai (T'ian-t'ai) Buddhism who composed the lectures in 6th century China. The method of Samatha Vipasyana meditation which came from India, was the subject of much longer treatise by Zhi Yi, called the *Maha-Samatha-Vipasyana* (*Da Zhiguan*). The shorter text of the "Little Manual of Vipasyana Meditation" became much more widely used, and is still popular today in Asia, where lay people and monks alike, not limited to the followers of Tendai (T'ian-t'ai) Buddhism, use the manual to practice Zen meditation.[1]

The book, written in a clear, terse style, is divided into ten concise chapters. Each chapter presents a plan of action to be followed by the reader. The language is lucid, the directions are explicit. The reader need not find a master to follow the text, though a spiritual director or guide is recommended for all who choose to follow a path of meditative prayer. Thus master and disciple are advised to use the manual together, as a guide to meditation.

The ten chapters are as follows:

1. Getting Ready. Five steps to purify the heart and mind must be taken before Zen meditation: "*Chanhui,*" repent all acts that may have offended or hurt others; use only simple food and attire; find a place to meditate; clear away irrelevant thoughts before meditation; and, choose a good teacher, and like-minded companions to meditate with.

2. Purify the five senses from desires and distracting images.
3. Purify the heart and mind from desires and distractions.
4. Harmonize mind, body, breathing, eating and sleeping.
5. Learn the five *Upaya* (convenient methods) for finding peace, and quelling selfish desires.
6. The practice of Zhi "Stop" and Guan "Look." (In two parts).
7. The proof of true Zen is compassion.
8. Learning how to recognize the demon Mara.
9. Zen teaches us how to heal.
10. Zen is for everyone, all religious systems.

These ten chapters give a clear and concise explanation of Samatha-Vipasyana, which literally means "Stop" "Look" Zen meditation. Samatha-Vipasyana are practiced while focusing attention on the body's physical center of gravity, the lower solar plexus, rather than the mind (concept and judgment) or heart (will). The intuitive powers are awakened, when the mind and heart are tranquil and still. In fact, the method is very close to the Taoist practice of centering on the "Lower Cinnabar Field," (*Xia Dantien*), the area located two inches below the navel and about three inches within, or midway between the fifth lumbar vertebrae and the front of the belly. This area is the true center of gravity of the human body. By focusing on this point, the mind is easily cleared of distracting images and judgments, and the heart is freed from extraneous desires. This is the basis for Zen meditation.

When doing Zen meditation, a state of quiet consciousness known today as "alpha state," is achieved. The harmone known as melatonin is excreted from the Pineal gland, the body is refreshed and rested. Healing is accelerated, the aging process is delayed, and awareness of the inner and outer worlds is enhanced. The true practitioner of Zen meditation is known for his or her ability to be compassionate, to heal, and to live peacefully and happily over a long period of life.

The brief introduction to the "little Manual" warns that those who practice Zen meditation without mastering Samatha (*Zhi*) cessation and Vipasyana (*Guan*) intuitive looking, are like a bird flying with one wing or a cart with only one wheel. Wisdom without compassion (the ability to heal and help others), creates a monster, a mad man. Compassion without wisdom makes for a foolish person. Compassion and wisdom together make the meditator fly with two wings, and ride straight on a two wheeled cart.

Thus the fruit of true Zen meditation makes one awaken to wisdom and compassion. The ordinary lay person who tries to practice Zen, can also increase concentration and therefore perfect some worldly skill (such as martial arts, painting or athletic competition) without practicing compassion. The person who takes the Bodhisattva vows, to help save all sentient beings (compassion without full realization of wisdom) still needs Zen meditation to fully understand the Buddha's main teachings (the Four Noble Truths, the Eight Fold Path).[2] Zen perfects both wisdom and compassion.

Tibetan Buddhism has expressed the close relationship between wisdom and Compassion by the graphic representation of a male and female Buddha in a close physical embrace. The grand protective deities of Tibet, Mahakala, Yamantaka, and a host of other quiet and wrathful images are depicted in tankha paintings and carved statues as united with a female consort. In this form of mystic symbolism the male represents compassion and the female wisdom. Both consorts are seen sometimes as ugly monsters, scaring us away from selfish desires, at other times as peaceful images in physical embrace. The images are not to be interpreted in the purely physical sense. Popular western publications not withstanding, in the true sense of Buddhist practice, the person who does Zen must be celibate if a monk or nun, monogamous if married. The symbol of male and female union, in the mystic sense, describes the harmonious blending of wisdom and compassion, a union to be attained through the meditation method of "stop" and "look" Zen.

Zhi Yi invites the reader to the practice of Samatha-Vipasyana Zen in ten straightforward, practical lectures. The instructions are written as a personal dialogue between the reader and the Zen master, rather than a learned treatise for scholars or experts. As such it has become a perennial favorite for teaching meditation in Asia.

---

1. Two English versions of the manual are available, the rendition of Lu K'uan Yü (Charles Luk) found in *The Secrets of Chinese Meditation* (New York: Samuel Weiser, Fifth Impression, 1979), pp. 109-160), and the more concise but incomplete translation of Kakuso Okakura, found in the *Harvard Theological Review*, Vol. XVI, No. 2, April 1923, pp. 71-87.

2. The Four Noble Truths: All life is conditioned by suffering; selfishness is the cause of suffering; annihilate selfishness; follow the way of compassion. The Eight Fold Path: 1) interdependent origin (I rely on all of nature, not myself, for my being; gratitude towards all for my conditioned existence); (2-6: no negatives) 2) see only good, 3) hear only good, 4) speak only good, 5) do only good, 6) think only good; 7) cessation of all judgment and concept, for meditative concentration; 8) compassion. Zen perfects these practices.

PROLOGUE
BUDDHISM AND ZEN

Zen is a word commonly used in western languages, often without knowledge of the Buddhist teachings upon which it is based, or the strict rules for its practice in Asia. For the reader unfamiliar with Zen and Buddhism, the following prologue gives a simplified account of their origins, as told in Asian and selected western sources.

For many in the western world Buddhism is equated with the practice of Zen. One reason is the many attractive books about Zen available in western book shops. The popular work of Alan Watts, (*The Way of Zen*, New York: Vintage Books, 1989) portrays Zen as something that any one can learn to practice. The equally respected, well read work of Philip Kapleau, *The Three Pilllars of Zen* (four hardback editions with John Weatherhill, Harper & Row, fourteen printings in paperback by Beacon Press, and the revised and expanded edition by Anchor Books, 1980) gives a detailed account of Zen as something that can be practiced by anyone resolute enough to do so.

The great Zen teacher D.T. Suzuki, whose works are perhaps the most widely read in the West, had no such sanguine views of foreigners or non-Japanese disciples who practice Zen. When asked by Shin'ichi Hisamatsu (while lecturing at Harvard in 1958) whether or not any foreigner had ever mastered Zen, or any foreigner had written anything truly useful about Zen, Suzuki replied that in fact no foreigner to his knowledge had the ability to do either of these feats, i.e., to practice or write about Zen.[1]

Suzuki and the Kyoto school of Zen scholars, (Nishitani, Nishida, and others), held that Zen was and is a peculiarly Japanese thing. Not even the Chinese as a people (aside from the noted Chinese monk-writers whose works on Zen are used extensively in Japan) had absorbed as the Japanese had the depths of Zen Culture, or so many in the Kyoto school of Zen believed.

From its beginning in China, Zen was practiced by every one who had the will and inspiration to do so. The Chinese text which is translated and paraphrased in these pages, the *Soshikan*, (Chn. *Xiao zhi guan*) a mid 6th century work that is still popular in Asia today, gives rules for practicing Zen that everyone can follow. Zen is not limited to or intended solely for Japanese use, in this earliest instruction manual from China.

Zen is only one of the many practices used by, but not limited to, Buddhism. It is a way not based on "faith," and not .limited to the Buddhist tradition.

Buddhism was founded by a historical person, Sakyamuni Buddha. His goal was to alleviate suffering, not found a religion. After his death a wide variety of doctrines, scriptures, and schools evolved, adapting his teachings into other cultures and nations. Buddhism became a "religion for export," for all practical purposes not widely practiced in the land of its origin.

To practice Buddhism one must "take refuge in" (i.e., accept) the *Three Precious Treasures (San Bao)*: the *historical Buddha*, his

---

1. See (Ed.) Donald Lopez, *Curators of the Buddha*, Chicago: University of Chicago Press, 1993, p. 133, for this reference; the citation is found in the chapter entitled "The Zen of Japanese Nationalism," by Robert H. Sharf.

basic *Dharma* (teachings), and the *Sangha* community of those who follow in his path.

Buddha was a real person who lived in the 6th-5th century B.C. Buddhism is the name given to his teachings, many of which were developed after his death. *Dharma* (Chn.: *fa*) means the Buddha's original teachings about enlightenment, later developments of his doctrines, and special "powers" attained through Buddhist or Taoist practice.[2]

From history we know that Buddha's given name was Siddhartha, and his family name Gautama. He is also called Sakyamuni, meaning "Sage of the Sakya clan." *Buddha*, which means "the awakened" or "the enlightened," was the name given him after his awakening.

Buddha taught that everybody is able to attain enlightenment, because "all living (sentient) beings have the Buddha nature," (i.e., the potency for enlightenment), and thus all may achieve Buddhahood. Later Buddhists taught that there were people who became Buddhas in the distant past, before Sakyamuni, as well as Buddhas who will appear in the future.

As time passed, the notion that there were many manifestations of the Buddha, past, present, and future, brought about the belief in multiple models for a Buddha, especially in the northern *Mahayana*, and related Tantric forms of practice. Buddhas were divided into three genre: 1) the historical Buddha, 2) the *Bodhisattva* or "enlightened beings" who seek to enlighten all others before achieving *parinirvana*, that is, the eternal shore, and 3) Buddhas who have crossed over to the other shore of boundless

---

2. For a study of Buddhism as a practice without belief, see Batchelor, Stephan, *Buddhism without Beliefs*, New York: Riverhead Books, 1997.

eternal light, such as Amida or Amithaba, from whence they enlighten others who invoke their name.

Thus there came to be three major schools of Buddhist practice: the *Theravada, Mahayana,* and *Tantrayana,* distinguished by geographic location and methods for achieving enlightenment. *Theravada* Buddhism, which emphasizes monastic and personal practice, is found in south and southeast Asia, mainly in Sri Lanka, Burma, Thailand, Laos, the China border with Laos and Burma, and Cambodia. *Mahayana* Buddhism is practiced in North and East Asia, mainly China, Korea, Japan, and Vietnam. *Chan* or Zen Buddhism is one of the two major forms of modern Mahayana practice. An even more popular Mahayana practice in Asia is "Pure Land" chant, i.e., the name of Amida, or some other form of the Buddha, is chanted to elicit faith in the enlightening power of Buddha. Pure Land is far more popular than Zen in Asia.

A lively inter-religious dialogue has taken place during the latter half of the Twentieth century between Buddhists and Christians, theologians and scholars. Zen (Chan) and to a lesser extent "name chant" methods have found resonance in Christian practice. Christians, both Protestant and Catholic alike, use and teach Zen methods in a purely Christian context. Zen is thus a contemplative method, not a belief system.

Tantrayana is found in Tibet, parts of Nepal, Mongolia, and Japan. It is defined by the concurrent use of *mudra* (hand symbols), *mantra* (Sanskrit chant) and *mandala* (centered visualization) for enlightenment. Tibet is the focus of Tantric practice today. It has become world famous due to the efforts of the Dalai Lama, leader in exile of the Yellow Hat (Gelugpa) school, to preserve all forms of Tantric practice both inside China and throughout the world. Besides the other major schools of Tantrism within Tibet, the

Tendai and Shingon schools of Japan preserve forms of Tantric prayer brought to Japan from Eighth century Tang Dynasty China. Today all Buddhists share the same philosophical theories.

Asian Buddhists consider the chanting of Sutras (prayer texts) much more important than the practice of Zen (quiet sitting). Some scholars of the Kyoto school even suggest that were it not for western interest and sales profits, Zen would not be as important in Japan as it is today.

Sakyamuni lived during the mid 6th-5th century B.C., slightly before and during the time of Confucius. He was the eldest son of the king of Kapilavastu, Suddhodana. His mother, Queen Maya, died soon after Buddha's delivery. Sakyamuni was brought up by his aunt (his mother's sister) Princess Prajapati. The legend surrounding Buddha's birth teaches that King Suddhodana hoped that Siddhartha, as heir to the throne, would be the long predicted "Wheel-turning King" (*Cakravartin raja*), that is, a "world ruler."

Legend also says that the flood of human suffering outside the gates of his father's palace touched him deeply. Sickness, old age, death were things he saw when walking through the city, away from the life of luxury behind the palace walls. All of his royal powers were insufficient to solve the problem of suffering. Only the life of a *Sadhu* (wandering ascetic) appealed to him. Buddha longed to forsake the throne and live the life of a monk.

But his father did not agree to his son's following the ascetic path, and ordered that he be confined within the palace walls, immersed in the pleasures of princely life. At the age of sixteen, by royal decree, Prince Siddhartha was married to Princess Yasodhara, who bore him a son named Rahula.

The Buddha could not be dissuaded. On a dark and moonless night, he rode his white horse out of the palace, shaved his head, and crossed over a river to live as a Sadhu in a forest. He lived together with other sadhu, his followers, for a period of six years, performing endless penitential exercise.

All manner of ascetic practice proved fruitless to alleviate the world's suffering or bring enlightenment. Buddha went alone to a *Pippala* (*Bo*) tree under which he sat in the "lotus" position, feet crossed under the body, facing to the east (rising sun, enlightenment). He vowed not to arise from this position until he had attained his goal of true awakening.

While under the *Bo* tree the demon Mara appeared to him, presenting a series of tempting images of worldly glory and sensual delight. It was during this vision that Buddha overcame the last demonic obstacle -- moral affliction (*klesa*). Pressing his right hand to the ground, he called on the earth goddess Privithi to witness his purity of mind and heart, and achieved complete enlightenment. Some believe, in retrospect, that the Buddha used a Zen like practice to achieve this awakening.

The enlightened Buddha accepted three pivotal theories of Bhraminic religion: "Inter-dependent Origin" (p*ratitya-samutpada*; dependence of all beings on each other for existence); "Karma," the law of cause and effect, (which influences our past, present and future); and, the six paths of transmigration to a new life after death (due to our Karmic or willed deeds).

The novelty of Buddha's teaching was to explain how liberation from the Bhraminic law of transmigration was possible. Bhramins taught that depending upon one's good or evil acts, one might be: reborn as a deva (heavenly being); a human being; an asura, a kind of militant deity, not much different from deva; an animal; as a hungry ghost (*preta*); or fall into hell and become a demon. By following Buddha's Four Noble Truths and Eight-fold

Path, we can be freed from this six-fold cycle of Bhraminic transmigration.

The basic teachings of the Buddha are the "Four Noble Truths" and the "Eightfold Path." The four noble truths are: all life is *suffering;* suffering's root is *selfish desire;* by totally *annihilating selfish desire,* one can follow a new way of life, an "enlightened" *path of compassion* for others.

The eightfold path to arrive at non-selfish compassion is equally direct. First, understand that I depend on all other things in the universe for my being. Thereupon, see, hear, say, touch, and think no evil about others. Finally, stop all verbal judgments of any kind, and contemplate all sentient beings with a true sense of selfless compassion. The eightfold path is the key to Zen practice.

The fundamental principle on which enlightenment is based is the first step of the eightfold path, the understanding of "Inter-dependent Origin" (*Pratitya-samutpada*). Every thing we see or know depends on a series of inter-related causes, conditions, and effects. Much of what we see as real, or imagine as troubles and worries, exists in our minds only. All worries are solved by thinking positive rather than negative thoughts, and finally by thinking no thought (making no judgments) at all. Once freed from self-centered thoughts, we can turn to a life of helping others.

Things we see around us can be real problems, such as natural or human catastrophes, physical and emotional suffering, all of which need some sort of intervention. To alleviate the effects of suffering, one must discover the causes and conditions that bring them about. All Buddhist doctrines therefore are ultimately derived from the theory of "Inter-dependent Origin."

Stupas (Chorten) found throughout East, Sc
Southeast Asia have enshrined as a verbal relic (*sarir*
Buddha the "inter-dependent origin" term as a poetic

Various dharmas (things) originate from *Hetu-pratyaya.*

With the diminishing of *pratyaya,* dharma ceases too.

My teacher, the Great Sramana (Buddha) thus spoke.

This *Gatha* (verse), is known as the *Dharmakaya Sarira Gatha* (relic of the historical Buddha's teachings in verse), because it is said to represent the basic doctrine left behind by the Buddha: "Whoever sees Inter-dependent Origin understands the Dharma, whoever sees Dharma sees Buddha."

The sacred verse provides four deeper insights into the Buddha's basic teachings:

1) The mind can only conceive what comes through the senses, i.e., *the mind cannot visualize an eternal, non-caused, immaterial being.*
2) There is no "self",(i.e., no permanent "I") *that is self-caused;*
3) *All things* or dharmas *are impermanent;*
4) Cause and effect relationships are continuous, *ever changing.*

The first term does not affirm or deny a transcendent "God," but rather the power of the intellect to visualize the existence of a transcendent being. It would be illogical and inconsistent to say that an absolute, Transcendent existence can be perceived by the mind, since the mind itself recognizes only what is caused, i.e., what comes from *hetu-pratyaya.*

It follows that one cannot conceive or predicate "caused being" of an *uncaused Absolute,* (something that all of the so-called "world" religions agree on). By accepting the theory of Inter-dependent Origin (*Pratitya-samutpada*), Buddhists must logically abstain from affirming or denying that the mind can perceive an absolute creator of the universe, as well as the ability of the mind to reject such a possibility, or achieve union with transcendent "non" being alone, by self will or self-achieved merit.

Though the person who accepts the theory of *Pratitya-samutpada* must logically refuse to affirm or deny an absolute first cause, by the same token he or she must oppose the belief that everything comes about by chance. There is no dharma (phenomenon) that arises without cause. All things that cease or arise are necessarily governed by the law of causality. It is formulated more succinctly in the following statement: "all things that arise necessarily have a cause."

Modern agnostics suggest that Buddhism in theory seems very close to atheism, if the theory of *Pratitya-samutpada* is to be taken literally. The Buddha taught not only that the notion of an Absolute could neither be affirmed or denied, but also refused to expound on an afterlife, the existence of a soul, or a heaven to which we go upon death.

Modern agnostic scholars not withstanding, the learned monks and nuns who follow Buddhist practice tend to favor the mystic, non-cognitive approach to the reality of an ultimate Transcendent, in the modern Buddhist-Christian dialogue, and reject agnostic or atheist interpretations of *Pratitya-samutpada.* Buddha himself did not deny the existence of the deities of Brahminism, teaching that they, too, were subject to the laws of Karmic recycling, like other sentient beings. All philosophical or theological discourse was avoided by Buddha.

With the passage of time the Buddha himself took on the role of a sort of deity, a *shen* or supernatural being, in popular religion. The Buddha brought peace as well as enlightenment, good fortune, blessing, healing, and other benefits in the present life. Sutras (Buddhist devotional texts) chanted by Buddhist monks

were thought to free souls from suffering in the purgatory-li'
of the afterlife, an overwhelming factor in Buddhism's succe.
throughout South, East, Southeast, and North Asia.

Thus from very early times Buddhism assumed a twofold way of spiritual perfection, that of the lay person who encountered the "Absolute" through the prayer of petition, and that of the ascetic who used the way of emptying (often called concept-and-judgment-free "apophasis," or "kenosis" in the west) as a form of interior prayer.

Zen Buddhism belongs to the latter kind of Buddhist practice, while devotional chant can belong to both forms, the way of petition for blessings, and as a practice for attaining apophatic awakening. In Asia, chant is considered to be a much easier way than the discipline of Zen sitting to achieve emptiness of heart and mind in prayer.

The debate about the existence of the soul, the meaning of "self" or "ego," the affirmation or denial of the existence of a Transcendent being, is not the stuff of which Zen practice is concerned. "Zen is for Everyone" (Chn. *Xiao Jr Guan*; Jpn. *Shoshikan*) explains in a very clear manner what Zen is about. We learn that compassion, not "winning an argument" is the proof of true Zen practice.

Acknowledgments

"Zen is for Everyone" is dedicated to the Rev. Ara Ryokan, of the Tendai Gakuin, Honolulu, Hawai'i, and to the late Ikuta Koken, Tantric master of Hieizan and Abbot of Bishamondo, Yamashina, Kyoto. It is due to their direction and support that the *Shobikan* text was made available to everyone as a tool to learn meditation. I am also grateful to Robert Campbell and Dennis Wyszynski for reading and suggesting many corrections in the manuscript. I am totally responsible for all errors and omissions in the text and the explanations.

The illustrations found throughout the book are from a set of wood block prints from the Zen painter Liang Kai (13th Century), found in a second hand book shop in Kunming, Yunnan province, China, on the way to Lake Luguhu, Zhongdian, and Muli, where Kagyu, Sagya, and Gelugpa monks perform long hours of Zen like meditation in the former area of Kham, Tibet. The prints, in the Chinese water color style, are reproduced in black and white here.

Michael Saso, August 22, 2000

1. GETTING STARTED

What are the *yüan* conditioned causes (*pratitya*)[1] for practicing Zen meditation? To practice "Stop, Look" (Samatha-vipasyana) style Zen meditation, five conditions must be fulfilled. The first is to keep the rules of purifying the body and mind. The second is to dress and eat properly. The third is to find a quiet place to meditate. The fourth is to free yourself from all sorts of extraneous worries. The fifth is to choose a good meditation teacher.

The first thing to do, for those who have set their minds and wills to practice "Stop" "Look" Zen meditation, is to keep the rules (Skrt.: *sila*; Chn.: *Jie*; Jpn.: *Kai*) concerning the purification of body and mind. As the Buddhist scriptures say, it is because of keeping the rules that all Zen (*dhyana*) meditation is born, suffering is destroyed and wisdom attained. This is why all monks and nuns must keep the precepts.

What are the ways in which the precepts are kept? There are three kinds of people who observe the rules. The first are those who before they became disciples of the Buddha did not commit the five deadly sins.[2] After they found a Buddhist master, they took the vows of triple refuge and the five rules,[3] thus making them disciples of the Buddha. If they left home and joined a monastery, they received the ten precepts (Sanskrit: *samaneras*) and the *upasampada* special rules,[4] thereby becoming great monks and nuns.[5]

If this sort of person receives and keeps the precepts, observing them in all purity, never breaking them in any way, they can be classified as the highest kind of practitioner. One must know that when this kind of person practices "Stop, Look" meditation, they will certainly realize the true Teachings of the Buddha, like a clean piece of white cloth that absorbs dye perfectly.

The second kind of practitioner is one who after promising to follow the precepts, does not break any of the more important rules, but as for the lesser precepts, commits many infractions. Such a person can practice samadhi ("stop", i.e., cessation) if according to the Dharma rules he or she performs acts of repentance and then is known for purity of observance. He or she is able to produce acts of *Samadhi* concentration and wisdom, like a piece of dirty cloth that can be washed clean and then will accept the dye.

The third kind of practitioner is made up of those who even though they have taken the vows to follow the rules, are unable to follow them with strong resolve and break all of the precepts, great and small. This class of practitioner must not follow the way of Theravada which does not provide a way of repentance for the four great transgressions (killing living things, stealing, sexual transgressions, and lying). Only if they follow the teachings of the Mahayana path can they do away with these obstacles. Therefore, the sutras say, there are two kinds of valiant contestants: those who never break the rules, and those who are able to reform themselves after their transgressions.

For those who wish to repent, it is necessary to observe to perfection the *Upasampada* (see note 4) and the ten laws. The ten Dharma laws are as follows:

1) A discerning belief in the law of cause and effect.
2) Awaken fear of causal consequences.
3) Elicit a deep sense of repentance.
4) Seek for ways to purify the self from all transgressions, as described in the Mahayana Sutras; once understood, the methods are strictly followed.
5) Public confession of all one's former transgressions.
6) Stop all mental imagery and judgments.

7) Firm decision to observe and protect the Buddha mind (wisdom and compassion).
8) Take the Great Vow of the Bodhisattva to save all sentient beings.
9) Always keep in one's consciousness the Buddhas of the Ten Directions.
10) See that sins themselves are not born, that transgressions are unsubstantial by nature.

If you can fulfill the above ten rules, then prepare the Meditation Hall (Jpn.: *Dojo*), wash and purify, put on clean clothes, burn incense and offer flowers, and while prostrating yourself in front of the "Three Precious Ones," (i.e., take refuge in the Buddha, Dharma and Sangha), perform the rites of repentance. Do this for three sets of seven day periods, or for seventy-seven days, or for three one-month periods, lasting over several years. When you have devoted your whole heart and mind to repentance for all of the serious transgressions committed, then you will attain to the total eradication and cessation of obstacles.

How do we know if our serious offenses have been totally purified and eradicated? You, the practitioner, will experience a sense of peace, uplifting body and mind while concentrating on the acts of repentance. Good dreams will occur. Manifestations of spiritual nature and other marvels will be seen. The heart will awaken and be open to good.

You will recognize, from within the self, while sitting (in Zen or Dhyana meditation), that the body becomes light, a cloud like image. From all of these practices you will gradually come to realize (attain) the state of Dhyana (Zen). After long practice, suddenly, enlightenment will arise in the heart-mind. A marvelous understanding of the Dharma's meaning will be achieved. Whenever the sutras are heard, you will grasp their meaning.

Because the heart-mind that delights in the Dharma is born, there will be no sorrow or regrets in the mind. So much so that all causes and conditions (you must realize), all the obstacles to the "Tao" (Margha, Buddha path) are destroyed, and all sins and transgressions are removed. From this time onward, you can keep the rules with firm resolve. Your fame will be for keeping the Sila (*shiluo*) precepts with great purity, and for practing Dhyana (Zen) meditation. It will be as if the dirty clothes were taken off, washed clean, and worn again, (after being) dyed to perfection.

If you have committed all of the serious offenses, and fear there is an obstacle to Dhyana meditation, even without putting on the robes of the monk and doing all the practices found in the sutras, you may still perfect all of the Dharma practices. All you need do is give birth interiorly to all sorts of acts of repentance, and in front of the Three Treasures (Buddha, Dharma, Sangha) admit all former transgressions, continuously cut off all images from the mind, discipline the body by constant sitting, see that sinful acts are by nature empty, and keep always in mind the Buddhas of the Ten Directions. (Thus sins will be cleansed, and vanish).

If you are a beginner in Zen (Dhyana) practice, then with an even firmer resolve bow and burn incense, repent and recite the precepts, and chant the Mahayana sutras. The obstacles to the Budda's path, and all your failings (sins) will gradually be wiped away, the Sila precepts kept in their purity, and Zen (Dhyana) meditation learned. Thus the *Miao Sheng Sutra* says:

> If you have committed all sorts of sins (transgressions), and your heart is filled with fear and unrest, and you wish to seek relief from these worries, there is no other way to be

rid of them than by practicing Zen meditation. You must find a secluded, quiet place, where one can purify the heart-mind and sit for a long time undisturbed. There, by chanting the Mahayana sutras, all your offenses will be cleansed, and all of the effects of Samadhi meditation will be yours.

The second condition: dress and food must be simple and sufficient. There are three kinds of dress (for the meditator to wear, according to his or her status). The first kind is used by the great masters of the Himalayan Snow Peaks (Tibet, Nepal). For them one garment that covers the body is sufficient, since they do not mingle with the world of men and are able to endure physical hardship. The second is for those who follow the path of *Dhuta* (i.e., the mendicant way), like Kasyapa (one of Buddha's first disciples). This class of person keeps only three garments, discarded by others. The third class of meditators are those who live in very cold countries (and all people) whose power of endurance is not high. The Tathagata (Buddha) allowed such people to keep 101 items besides the three garments of the mendicant. For them the important thing is cleanliness, to know what is sufficient, to know contentment, and to realize that to eat too much or covet things disturbs the mind and obstructs the Buddhist way (of wisdom with compassion).

As for food, there are four kinds of diets to follow: first, the great masters who live in the hills, away from the world, eat herbs, fruits and vegetables, whatever that can be found (in nature) that nourishes the body. The second kind of diet is that followed by those who observe the mendicant way, and do not practice the four kinds of unlawful living for monks. Because they live only on food acquired by begging, they are able to show forth in their lives the saintly path (of the Buddha), and thus are named "disciples of the holy one." Note that there are four unlawful ways to support oneself (for monks) as follows: "eating with mouth downward," i.e., growing and *selling* medicinal herbs; "eating with mouth up," or practicing fortune telling and astrology (star-gazing); "eating with mouth pursed," living by sweet words and flattery; and "eating with squared mouth," divination and sorcery. Sariputra (one of Buddha's disciples) taught lady Jingmu that these were evil ways to make a living.

The third is living by *Aranya*, the food offerings put on the altar by pious folk, which are afterwards given to the monks for their livelihood. The fourth is eating peacefully within the monastic community of monks. To live this ways is called "fulfilling the conditions for sufficient food and dress." Why so? Because if one doesn't fulfill these conditions, not living thus, the heart is not at peace and the Buddha way (compassionate wisdom) is impeded.

The third causal-condition is living quarters (place of abode), i.e., living in a secluded quiet retreat. A retreat is a place where one is not busy about many things, and a "quiet place" is where no noise or trouble reaches. There are three kinds of places where Zen meditation can take place. The first is in secluded mountains, far from the abode of men. The second is in the community of mendicant monks, three or four miles from inhabited villages, where the sound of grazing animals is not heard, far from worldly cares or troubles. The third is inside the *Aranya* (a quiet monastery-like place), which is (set aside for meditation) undisturbed by visitors or guests. All such places fulfill the requirements of retreats and quiet undisturbed places (for doing Zen meditation).

The fourth causal condition: Occupations to be avoided: relinquish all occupations which are solely for earning money, and other forms of selfish employment for profit. Leave behind all social relationships, running after friends, relatives, and involvement in secular affairs with worldly people. Relinquish secular art, preoccupation with the world of technology, medicine, conjuration, fortune telling and accounting. Leave off all vain scholarly pursuits, reading, chanting, listening to and studying the classics, and distracting mental activities. This is called "discarding all conditional affairs." The reason is because while these things are being done the practice of the Buddha path is impeded, the heart is disturbed and the mind is difficult to control.

The fifth causal condition. Keep company with people of compassionate minds. There are three kinds of good people: the first is the person who looks after your external needs, providing food and sustenance, and protecting you without disturbing your peace. The second is a person who goes along with you mutually walking the same path without disturbing your practice. The third is the knowledgeable master, who is skilled in internal and external *upaya* skills of Buddhist Zen meditation, imparting the teachings to you in such a way that you benefit and are filled with joy. When you have understood the above, the five conditions for practicing "Stop" "Look" Zen are fulfilled.

---

1. The word *Yuan* (Jpn.: *En*, Sanskrit: *pratitya*) means a condition or relationship, rather than a cause (*Yin;* Jpn.: *in*, Sanskrit: hetu). This first chapter treats of the *yuan* or proper conditions for performing Zen meditation.

2. The Five Deadly Sins (*wu ni*, Jpn. *Gogyaku*) are: to kill one's mother, one's father, a monk, to make a Buddha bleed, to cause dissension.

3. The Three Refuges are the Buddha, Dharma (teachings) and Sangha community of believers). The Five Precepts of the laity are: not to steal, not to kill, not to commit adultery, not to lie and not to drink intoxicants.

4. The 255 rules for monks, 348 precepts for nuns.

5. Ten precepts of the monastery: to the first five precepts add: abstain from bodily perfume and luxury, singing and dancing, sleeping in a large bed, eating out of the assigned times, keeping money or jewelry.

2. QUELLING DESIRES

The cravings or desires which are to be quelled or overcome are five in number. Those of you who wish to do Zen sitting and practice "Stop" and "Look" meditation must quell these five desires. The five cravings are the sights, sounds, smells, tastes and touches of the secular world, which give rise to "erotic love", i.e., the heart's confusion and attachment to all sorts of things. If you can know in depth your past transgressions and no longer associate with the occasion of repeating them, this is called "emptying desire."

The desires which pertain to "rupa" (form, color) are those which men and women elicit by beauty of face and smartness of figure, clear eyes, trimmed eyebrows, rouge lips, white teeth, adorned with things treasured by the worldly, blue, red, yellow, white, scarlet, purple, bright green and all sorts of vivid colors, a source of delight to foolish people, the very sight of which elicits erotic desires and the doing of evil deeds. Such a person was King Bimbisara, who, tainted by lust, ran into enemy country in pursuit of the courtesan Ambapali and was caught in her bed chamber.[1] The same was true of King Udayana, who out of infatuation and lust, cut off the hands and feet of 500 ascetics.[2] Even though they had so many causal conditions (inhibiting meditation), they were able to recognize their transgressions of *rupa* lust due to sight, as stated in the *Awakening of Faith in Mahayana.*[3]

Cravings arising from sound include the sound of harp, lute, harpsichord, flute, musical sounds produced from strings, bamboo, metal, stone, men and women singing, hymns, odes, and all such melodies that when heard influence the common people and lead them to do evil deeds. Such was the case with the 500 ascetics of the snow mountains (Himalayas) who when they heard the singing of Lady Kandara, lost their powers of Zen concentration, their mind and hearts led astray and confused.[4] Even though they had so many causes and conditions inhibiting meditation, still they were able to recognize their transgressions due to sounds heard, as is stated in the *Awakening of Faith in Mahayana.*

Desires arising from the sense of smell are: perfume used by men and women on the body, worldly drinks, foods, fragrances and all sorts of incense and aromas, which when the foolish inhale, opening up the gateways to lust. Such was the case with a young monk who, when standing by a pond of blossoming lotuses, was overcome with the fragrance of the flowers. Feelings of erotic love sprang up in his heart, which caused the spirit of the pond to scold the monk mightily. "How dare you take the fragrant breath from my flowers, and use it to open yourself to all sorts of desires that lay dormant within you?" Even though there were many causes and conditions inhibiting him from meditation, he recognized that the sense of smell was a cause for transgression, as is stated in the *Awakening of Faith in Mahayana.*

Desires arising from the sense of taste are: the bitter, sour, sweet, stringent and salty, all sorts of food and drink, gourmet banquets and exotic flavors, that lead astray, taint the heart, and give rise to evil deeds. Such was true of a young monk who had an inordinate fondness for butter. After his death he was reborn as a bug floundering in butter. But even with so many causal conditions as these, one can recognize that the sense of taste leads to transgressions, as is stated in the *Awakening of Faith in Mahayana.*

Desires arising from the sense of touch are: the bodies of men and women, soft, smooth, delicate and supple, warm in winter and cool in summer; all those enthralled by the sense of touch, foolish people without wisdom, who have fallen into a deep pit, an obstacle to the deeds of the Buddha path. Such was the case of the hermit called "One Horn" (Ekasrnga, i.e., Dokkaku or Ikkaku Sennin).[5] Because of his lust he lost his spiritual powers and was seduced by a courtesan who put her foot on his neck. Even in spite of such conditions and causes, he was able to recognize his transgressions due to the sense of touch, as it is said in the *Awakening of Faith in Mahayana.*

You (the disciple) ask, "How to quell the five desires?" The answer is given in the *Awakening of Faith in Mahayana.* Alas! Sentient beings, though troubled by these five desires still never get enough of them. The five desires have no real pleasure in them, playing with the heart, making it evil, like kindling for fire, its smoke swirling and beclouding. The five desires never satiate, like a dog gnawing a dry bone. They bring strife, like birds fighting over a piece of raw meat. They are a contrary wind that blows a torch into the face of humans. They are like a venomous serpent that bites when trodden on.

The five senses bear no fruit, unreal as things found in a dream, transitory as a spark struck from flint. People of the world are foolish, coveting the five senses until they die, not realizing how much endless suffering they bring in later lives.

The five desires are what humans have in common with animals. All sentient beings experience the five senses, enslaved by their cravings. Those who follow these depraved desires are cycled into the three lower paths (preta, asura, demon)[6]

We have now begun the way of Zen cultivation. These desires are veiled obstacles, great thieves which must be quickly left behind, as is said in the Zen Sutra:

Life and death have no end, due to sense desires.
Nursing feelings of hate, we are buried,
Impelled to receive all sorts of anguish.
The body smells like a rotting corpse,

Defiled by the filth flowing from its cavities.
Like worms reveling in toilet feces,
Are the foolish minded who know this not.
The wise must see the body (as it is).
Not sullied by the pleasures of the world.
Not attached, without desires, this is true nirvana,
Just as all Buddhas say, walk with one heart, one mind.
Count your breaths when meditating,
This is called to practice the way of the recluse.

---

1. Bimbisara, Fifth king of the Saisnaga dynasty of Maghada, later became a follower of the Buddha. Hee was deposed by his son, and died in jail. See Inagaki (1988, p. 12.)

2. King Udayana, ruler of the Kingdom of Kausambi, also became a follower of Buddha after a life in pursuit of lustful desires. He became ill when the Buddha was absent, and could only be healed by having a sandalwood statue of the Buddha made to recall his likeness. A copy of this statue is said to be kept in Shoryoji, Sada, Kyoto. See Inagaki, p. 353.

3. The *Makaen-ron*, or *Makakishinron*, attributed to Asvaghosa, of which there are two translations into Chinese, Paramartha's (TT.32, No. 1666) and Siksananda's (TT. 32, No. 1667); see Inagaki, p. 32.

4. Kimnaras, the eight female defenders of Buddhism, demigods of music, half human and half demon who act as protective deities.

5. A previous incarnation of Buddha, he was born of a female deer in the mountains of Baranasi, with the appearance of a man but a single horn growing out of his head. He was seduced by a beautiful woman named Senta, said to be Buddha's wife Yasodhara in a previous life. See Inagaki, p. 122.

6. The six paths of recycling existence are deva, human, animal, preta (orphan soul), Asura, and demon. Buddhist enlightenment frees the soul from the cycling process.

3. ELIMINATE IMPEDIMENTS

There are five impediments to be eliminated. These are: internal desires, anger, slumber, restless remorse, and doubt.

The first impediment to Zen meditation is desire. In the above chapter we spoke of desires arising from the external world. Here we shall discuss internal images that give rise to desire. When you become a practitioner of Zen sitting and meditation, you will feel in your heart various desires which the more you think about them, the more they burden the compassionate heart. In order that such thoughts not arise, you must awaken inwardly to the need to eradicate them.

An example of this is the fisherman Gipaka (Juppaka). So strong were the desires that arose from his heart that his body was consumed in flames.[1] So much the more, if desires are born in your heart, how will they not burn away compassion and Dharma too? Those who are filled with desires leave the Buddha path far behind. Thus, desire is the source of much turmoil and disorder within. If your heart is filled with desires, there is no way to approach the Dao (Path of Buddhist meditation). As for eliminating desires, a hymn (Gatha) relates:

> If you repent and enter the Buddha path,
> Holding the alms bowl to bless all sentient beings,
> How can you tolerate being sullied by desires,
> Deeply caught up in the five emotions?
> Having dispelled the five desires for pleasure,
> Casting them off and no longer concerned,
> How can you still want to arouse desire,
> Like a fool who eats one's own vomit.
> All desires when elicited bring sorrow,

When attained bring fear and dread (of loss),

When lost nurture fiery irritation.

All these are times without joy;

All desires bring such misfortune.

Thus if you can dispel them,

You will attain the deep joy of Zen meditation,

No longer seduced or fooled.

Thus by such conditions and causes, void yourself of obstructive desires, as is said in the *Awakening of Mahayana* texts, the Gatha for suspending desires.

The second impediment to Zen meditation is Anger. It is the root that causes all compassionate Dharma (all good Dharma) to be lost. Heeding anger is the conditioning cause for following an evil path, the enemy of joy in the Dharma (Buddhist way), robber of the compassionate heart, cache for all kinds of malevolent words.

When the practitioner does Zen sitting, his/her mind is filled with thoughts of how this person hates me, and hates my loved ones, how he delights in my distress. My thoughts are flooded with past and future events, which when mulled over, cause the nine kinds of distress. Worry causes anger, anger hate, and hate makes us want to take vengeance on others. Feelings of hatred fill the heart, and thus are called an impediment (to Zen meditation). Hatred must be expelled at once, and not allowed to nurture and grow.

Thus Indra (Taishaku) once asked Buddha in a hymn (Gatha):

What kills inner peace, what destroys inner joy,

What poison, when swallowed, destroys compassion?

The Buddha answered in a hymn (Gatha):

Kill anger, then feel inner peace;

Kill anger, there will be no inner grief.

Anger is the source of poison;

Destroy anger; all will be compassion.

If you know this thoroughly, you must by compassion and patience eliminate anger, leading the heart into peace and tranquility. Thus is it said in the *Awakening to Mahayana* text. The Buddha taught his disciples this hymn to eliminate anger, something which must be extensively explained and carefully followed.

The third impediment to Zen meditation is slumber. When the inner heart and mind are darkened, this is called interior slumber. When darkness enshrouds the five senses, the limbs and joints are fatigued, one is ready for bed and sleep. This is cause and condition for sleeping during meditation, which state is called the impediment of slumber. It destroys the fruits and joys of the present and the future worlds.

Because of this wicked state, the worst of all evils is produced. How can these added impediments, feelings and urges be got rid of, when sleep makes one like a dead person? There is nothing that one can be aware of, because one is not awake. It is thus difficult to get rid of or eliminate any obstacles when sleeping.

There once was a Bodhisattva who taught his disciples how not to sleep, saying:

> Awaken, all of you, do not sleep while embracing your stinking corpse. You have a serious illness that can be transmitted to other people, a serious sickness from an arrow that has entered the body. All sorts of sorrow and suffering have arisen, how can you sleep?
>
> You are like a person bound and about to be slain, calamities about to befall you, how can you doze? The culprit is bound but not destroyed. The danger is not yet crushed, like living in the same room with a venomous snake. It is like

being in battle with swords clashing around you. How can you be sleeping at such a time!

Sleeping is like being in a great darkness, where nothing can be seen. Every day you are deceived, human intelligence deranged. If one uses sleep to cover the mind, then nothing can be known. If there is such great loss, how can you slumber? If there are so many conditional causes to eliminate, if the impediment of sleep and the time of awakening are not regular, then cut short your sleep, force yourself not to be covered with confusion. If layers of confusion cover the heart-mind, you must use Zen awakening and the Zen staff, and so forth, to overcome it.

The fourth impediment is restless remorse. There are three kinds of restlessness (i.e., instability and inconstancy which lead to later remorse). The first is restlessness of the body. The second is restlessness of the mouth. The third is restlessness of the heart.

Restlessness of the body is seen when you like to travel and roam about, sporting and jesting, and are uneasy when sitting. Restlessness of the mouth is when you like singing and chattering, debating whether something is true or not without any commitment to one side or the other, and all sorts of secular talk.

Restlessness of the heart occurs when your mind and emotions are scattered, images and ideas are allowed free access to your mind, such as when one is absorbed in worldly literature, arts and talents, and the stimulation of evil concepts and images. This is what is called a restless mind.

If restlessness becomes your way and path, the heart as your inner home is shattered. If the heart is dissipated and not settled (i.e., in Samatha, a single focus, concentration during meditation), how much the more is (the mind) restless and scattered. It is like a drunken elephant unchained, a camel without a nose ring, that cannot be stopped or controlled. Thus a Gatha declares:

> You monks who have already shaved your heads and dyed your clothes,[2] carried your earthenware bowls and begged for food, how can you take joy in secular play, the restless way? In loosening your feelings, you have lost any benefit from the Dharma.

That is to say, you have lost any profit from the Buddhist way, and derive no real joy in worldly things. When you realize that this agitated state is an offense (to bodily and mental peace), you must quickly reject it.

As for remorse, if you are restless but do not regret (the choice of the Zen Buddhist way), then feeling restless is not of itself an impediment. Why so? When you feel restless, you are not yet in the realm of conditioned causality.[3] Only afterwards, when desires enter, while doing Samatha meditation, and one begins to regret what one chose before (the Buddha path), then anxiety and resentment flood the heart; at this point there is an impediment.

However, remorse is of two kinds. The first is when restlessness causes later regrets, as was stated above. The second is when a person who has committed offenses continually worries and frets about them, in which case remorse is like an arrow lodged in the heart so firmly that it cannot be removed. A Gatha of the Buddha says:

> Things you shouldn't do, those you do. Things
> You should do, those you don't. Remorse, anxiety
> Are fires that burn. Thus, in a future world you will
> follow evil ways. If you can repent shortcomings,
> Repentance wipes away repeated worry.

If your heart takes joy in serenity,
There's no need to worry ever again.
It's as if there are two kinds of regrets,
Not doing what we should have done,
Doing what we should not have done;
Such worries make you look like a fool.
It's because we don't have regrets in our heart-mind
That the things we didn't do we are able to do,
And all the evil things we have done,
Cannot keep us from doing what we should do now.

If all of these causes and conditions are present, and you void yourself of the impediment of restless regret, your heart will become pure and tranquil, and the impediment will not come back.

The fifth obstacle to be removed is that of doubt. The reason why doubts recur is because with all of your Dharma practices you do not have the Buddha mind-heart.[4] The reason why you don't have the Buddha mind is because all of your Buddhist practices were barren and nothing was achieved.

For instance, you are like a person who entered a treasure-filled mountain, but had no hands, so nothing could be picked up. By repeating this experience many times (attaining nothing from meditation), you are filled with doubts, and there will necessarily be many obstacles to Zen meditation.

Here let us state the obstacles to Zen meditation. There are three kinds of obstacles: doubts arising from the self, doubts arising from the master, and doubts arising from practice (of the Zen way of meditation).

The first obstacle is to have doubts about yourself. If you say over and over to yourself "I am a stupid, dull person, my sins are sullying, deep and dirty, no one else is as bad as I." If you're able to generate this kind of self doubt, you will never develop Zen practice. If you want to get rid of these doubts, then don't make so little of yourself, since the good deeds in past worlds are just as innumerable (useless and hard to measure).

The second is to doubt your master. "He may have a sense of decorum and fine appearance, but toward me he doesn't have any respect. How can he teach me?" If you are filled with such doubts and indignation, it will be an obstacle to Zen meditation. If you seek a way to get rid of this hindrance, do as the *Mahayana Awakening* says:

He (the Master) is like a fetid bag filled with gold.

If the gold inside is precious, don't throw away the bag.

We practitioners are the same; even if the master is not very clean, when sitting in front of him we should think of him as the Buddha. This kind of thing is explained very clearly and concretely in the scriptures, which examples must be taught far and wide.

The third is to doubt the very teachings and way of the Buddha itself. People of the world usually champion their own viewpoint, and whatever other way is introduced, they do not believe it. Even if you respectfully accept and practice it, if some doubts arise, then the Dharma has not yet penetrated to the heart. Why is this so? If there are doubts, the Gatha explains (how to eliminate them) as follows:

> When we come to a forked road, and doubt which one to follow, so with all Dharma, real and phenomenal, doubts will arise again and again. If you don't thoroughly seek the cause of these (many) misgivings, doubts of the real and phenomenal, doubts about all Dharmas will be born of (your) foolishness. Evil comes from evil, compassion from true Dharma. (Avoid) what is not from compassion, through life, death, and nirvana too. Zen meditation has its own true

Dharma path, from the midst of which doubts cannot arise. If you harbor doubts and worries, the King of death will send his messenger from hell to bind you. Like a lion catching a deer, there is no escape from him.

Even though there are doubts in the world, you must follow the wondrous way of compassion, just as when looking at the fork in the road, you should follow the one with most profit for you. Putting it another way, to enter into the way of the Buddha, it is necessary to have trust. If you don't have trust, even if you've chosen the Buddha path, in the end you will have attained nothing. If you have so many causal conditions, and awaken to the knowledge that doubts are transgressions, you must quickly be rid of them.

You ask me, "We are in the dusty way of no compassion, without measure or boundary, how then can we cast off the five impediments?"

I answer, "Within these five obstacles one can in fact distinguish three poisons which can be considered to be the roots, from which arise 84,000 (mental and physical) afflictions, the gateway to all the sullied glory (of the world).

"The first of these is the impediment of greedy desire, i.e., the poison of greed. The second impediment is anger, that is, the poison of anger (hatred and vengeance). The third impediment is sloth and doubt, two results of the poison of stupidity."

The causes of the five obstacles are in fact the three poisons (greed, hatred, stupidity). Thus it is said that there are three poisons. The three poisons infect the impediment of restless or indecisive remorse, splitting into four kinds of mental affliction. Each kind of affliction has 21,000 manifestations, which multiplied by four makes 84,000. For this reason by destroying the five obstacles, we rid ourselves of all feelings lacking in compassion.

The person who practices Zen, even if burdened with all sorts of conditional causes, does in fact cast off the five impediments. It is like a person freed by paying off a debt, the healing of a serious illness, a hungry beggar coming into a wealthy kingdom, or being saved from a band of evil robbers, such is the peace attained when this distress is no more.

You the practitioner will find this so too. If you rid yourself of these five obstacles, your heart will be peaceful and undisturbed, your mind clear and joyful. It is like the sun and moon that also have five affairs that obstruct their light, i.e., smoke, clouds, dust, fog, and the Rago Asura (demon) who causes eclipses.[5] Because of them sun and moon cannot give light. The human heart is obstructed in the same way.

---

1. Gipaka was a fisherman who fell in love with a princess. The Buddhist legend says that his heart was so consumed with the fires of lust that he died of the heat, like an inward fire covered with ashes. See Sekiguchi (Tokyo: 1978), p. 37.

2. The Buddhist monks of ancient India were required to shave their heads and dye their Kesa robe a brown color. See Sekiguchi (1978, p. 38).

3. That is, the feelings themselves are not impediments to the Buddha way, nor to the practice of Zen. Only when one deliberately entertains or mulls over the feelings, and thereby regrets having left worldly ways, does the causal condition of an impediment arise.

4. Jpn. *Shinshin*, the believing heart, is identified with *Honshin*, the Buddha mind, or one's original mind, the Buddha nature. See Inagaki, p. 304, and p. 110.

5. The Rago Asura or (Sanskrit) Rahula, is a mythological creature who is said to eat the sun and moon, thus causing eclipses. He is popular in Tibet. See Inagaki, p. 241-2.

4. HARMONY

The word harmony is used here in the sense of harmonizing the five (Dharma) activities. The first is to regulate the times for eating and drinking. The second is to regulate sleeping, the third to regulate the body, the fourth to regulate breathing, and the fifth to regulate the heart-mind.

To explain why this is necessary, let us take an example from something near at hand, which applies even more to these regulations (for meditation). It is like a potter in the secular world, who when he aspires to make all sorts of pottery, must first knead and prepare his clay carefully so that it is neither too hard nor too soft, and only then may he shape it on the wheel.

It is also like playing the lute (qin); one must first tune the strings, so that they are neither too loose nor too tight, and only then can the musician play it, and make beautiful melodies.

If you the practitioner (of Zen) wish to purify your heart, you must follow the above examples. To finely attune the five Dharma activities, you must harmonize them in a manner befitting the practice of Samadhi (Samatha, or Zen meditative concentration).[1] If there is some aspect that has not been regulated, it will be hard for you to overcome the many obstacles (to meditation), or difficult for good roots to put forth shoots.

The first thing you must do is regulate the intake of food, that is, eating becomes a part of Dharma practice, something which assists the body to enter the Dharma path. Food when over indulged causes the Qi energy to become hard pressed and the body listless, the arteries and veins obstructed, the heart closed off, not at peace when sitting in meditation. If you eat too little, then the body will be tired and the heart hung up, the mind's thoughts unsteady. If both of these (over eating and insufficient nourishment) are eliminated, then one can attain to the way of Zen concentration. In addition to this, if you eat dirty and sullied things, your heart will become giddy and confused. If you eat things hard for the body to digest, then you will feel sick when moving and resting, and the four great things to be avoided will be overturned.[2] This is what is called beginners' Zen. You must plumb its depths. Thus, the Buddhist canon says:

> When the body's at peace, the (Zen) way is enriched.
> When eating and drinking, know what's sufficient,
> Take joy in a life of quiet seclusion,
> The heart filled with joyful peace is energy laden.
> This is what is called the teaching of all Buddhas.

The second thing to regulate is sleep. Sleep is a time of darkness and doubt, which should not be indulged in. If you sleep too much, you not only waste time which could be spent in refining sacred meditation, you also lose precious time for Gongfu (kungfu) practice,[3] and lead the heart-mind into darkness. If the roots of compassion are not deep, the first awakening to enlightenment will not be lasting. Regulating sleep makes spirit and breath pure and clean, and the heart bright and peaceful. If you can do this, your heart-mind will enter the realm of the sacred and samadhi (concentration achieved in Zen meditation) will be manifest in you. Thus, the Buddhist canon says:

> If during the first night watch and the last night watch[4] you waste your time, and do not during this time control sleep, due to such causal conditions you will pass through your whole life empty, and nothing will be attained. You must consider the fact that an inconstant flame consumes all the many worlds, which you must free yourself from as early as possible, by not overindulging in sleep.

The third, fourth and fifth things to regulate are the body, the breath and the heart-mind. Since these three faculties are used together, they cannot be treated separately. Since there is a beginning, middle, and ending to the practice of meditation, there is a relative difference in how one enters into, abides in, and comes out of Zen contemplation.

When entering Zen meditation the first thing which you the practitioner must do is, if you wish to enter *Samadhi* (mental state of concentration focusing on one object) is to properly regulate the body. This must be done outside the state of meditation. Working, resting, walking, stopping, in motion or rest, whatever you do, you must in all things choose with care and discretion.

If your actions are coarse and rough, then your breath and Qi energy will follow in accord, i.e., your Qi energy will become coarse, the heart-mind will be dissipated and hard to control, and when it's time to sit in meditation you'll find it a bother, the heart will not be at peace. Because of this, even when you are outside the state of meditation, you must still use your heart-mind in a way not contrary to the "skillful means" (*Upaya*) of meditation.

When beginning to meditate, it is necessary to make the body quite comfortable and at ease, in a suitable place. (Thus) at the beginning (of the meditation) go to the woven chairs (set aside for Zen practice), and adjust the cushion on it so you can sit comfortably for a long time without undue hindrance.

Next, you must attend to your feet. If you sit in the half-lotus position, put the left leg over the right leg, and pull the left foot back until the toes rest on top of the right knee, and the right foot is under the left knee. If you want to sit in the full lotus position, then place the right leg over the left, and tuck the sole of the feet up from under the right.

Then, adjust the belt and monk's robes a bit so that they are neat and won't come undone when meditating. Next, attend to your hands. Lay the left hand, palm up, on top of the right palm, with the thumbs slightly touching. Place both palms thus held together on top of the left leg, and pull the two hands toward the body so that they come to rest beneath heart (bringing calming peace to the heart).

Next, regulate the body by moving backward and forward and flexing the limbs and joints seven or eight times, as one does in self massage, not letting arms and legs lean unevenly. Continue to adjust the body, by sitting up straight, keeping the back erect without sagging to the front or back. Then adjust the head and neck, so that the tip of the nose lines up with the belly button, bending neither left or right, held neither too low or too high, face even and body settled properly.

Now open your mouth and exhale all impure Qi breath from the chest. The method of expelling the breath is: open the mouth and exhale breath, and as you let it go, see with your mind all of the divisions of the body, all of the blockages in the channels of the body, to be expelled with the breath as you exhale.

When done, close the mouth, and inhale pure clean air through the nose. Repeat this process three times. But if your body and breath are well regulated, once is enough.

Next you must close your mouth, letting the lips and teeth just barely touch, and bending the tongue up toward the roof of the mouth (the hard palate) but not quite touching it. Then close your eyes slightly, so that a little light still comes in.

At this point you must sit straight in the Zen position, just as if you were a stone, not letting the head, body or limbs move. This is how when entering Zen meditation you are to regulate your body.

To sum it all up in a few words, the body should not be too loose or too rigid, if you want to keep the body regulated.

The second step when entering Zen meditation is to regulate the breathing. In doing so there are four ways to breathe, i.e., the breath sounds like wind blowing, sighing, Qi flowing, and quiet breathing. The first three are not appropriate for adjusting your breath, while the last one does help regulate it.

Why is the first way called "windy?" Because the breath as it enters and leaves your nose makes a sound like wind blowing. When is breathing called "sighing?" When exhaling and inhaling are uneven in length, even if there is no sound, this condition is called sighing.

What is "Qi flowing" breath? When, while sitting, your breathing, though it makes no sound and is even, is still rough and energy-filled (i.e., filled with Qi energy, not refined), this is called "Qi" breath.

Quiet Zen breathing occurs when there is no sound, not broken, not coarse. Exhaling and inhaling are refined (continuous like a fine thread spinning), aware yet unaware of the breathing process. Body at peace, the feelings become quiet and contented. This condition is called quiet (Zen) breathing.

Windy breath scatters, sighing binds, Qi breath tires, quiet breath settles (you) into the Zen meditative state. If when sitting you breathe in the windy or any of the first three "non-regulated" ways, and try to meditate, your heart will be troubled and your mind hard to focus.

If you wish to regulate (your heart-mind), there are three techniques that you must rely on. The first is to focus your attention on the lower part of the abdomen (three inches or so below the navel, two or three inches within, the center of gravity of the body).

Second, you must relax the body entirely. Third, you must visualize your breath as passing through every pore of your body, going out and entering every joint and crevice, so that there are no obstacles to its even flow.

If you purify your heart-mind and make the breath quiet and hardly perceptible, then when the breathing is thus regulated, worries and anxieties will not arise and the mind will be easily focused and settled.

The above defines what the practitioner does when first entering Zen meditation, i.e., the means to regulate breathing. To sum it up, essentially to regulate breathing don't breathe too tensely or too loosely.

The third step to take when entering Zen meditation is to regulate the mind. There are two things to remember here. The first is to quell all random images, not letting them pass through your mind freely, and not allowing them room to float or sink in. The second is to keep the heart-mind from being too deep, too shallow, too lax or tense a condition.

What is meant by too deep a condition? If when you are sitting the mind falls into a twilight or dark state and begins to lose its awareness, the head nods and sinks forward, this is called too deep a condition. At this point you should visualize an imaginary object at the tip of the nose, and force the mind to become aware of it, not letting yourself be distracted by random images. This will control the mind from sinking too deep.

What is meant by the shallow or floating condition? If while you are sitting in Zen meditation the heart-mind likes to move about freely, and the body becomes restless, and you visualize and recall unusual external objects, this is called the shallow or floating state.

At this time it is easy to quell the heart mind by focusing attention down into the lower abdomen, and make it (the solar plexus) an object of vision. You thus control all random thoughts, keeping your mind settled in Zen concentration. In this way your heart is serene and tranquil.

You ask me "In such a condition isn't it easy for the mind to become too relaxed or too tense?"

My answer is that yes, sometimes indeed this does occur. When you try to concentrate too quickly, fervidly using the mind while sitting, focusing attention toward some conceptual image, you thereby cause the thought to enter into your (mind's) concentrated gaze, thus forcing the Qi energy upwards, causing the chest and mind to ache.

When this happens, loosen and free the heart's attention, visualizing the Qi energy to flow downward (to the belly), and thereupon the tension will subside of itself.

If the heart is in a slack state, you will perceive that the attention wanders and the will power flows away, the body's strength ebbs, the mouth salivates, and sometimes darkness will overpower the mind. In such a case you must get hold of your body, control your thoughts, bring the heart-mind back to the state of awareness by focusing on the belly, to master yourself.

You must use these means to control slackness. Thus one can know the tightness or slackness of the heart-mind by the foregoing analysis, which shows the way to regulate the heart when beginning Zen meditation.

In summary, entering Zen concentration is basically passing from the coarse to the refined. I.e., the body is coarse, breathing is in between, and the heart is the most refined. By regulating the coarse so that it is refined, the heart becomes peaceful. These, then, are the *Upaya* (skillful means) to begin Zen meditation.

Next we must talk about what to do while sitting in Zen meditation. The same three things must be attended to. In one sitting, whether the time is long or short, i.e., within a twelve hour period whether it lasts for one, two, or three hours, when using one's heart mind to regulate thoughts, one must know well during this time whether or not to harmonize body, breath and heart.

Thus when you are sitting, when you seek to regulate the body according to its present condition, seeing how it is at this moment, whether too loose or too tight, leaning or bent, head held too low or too high, you feel that accordingly you should straighten up, each time you do this it brings peace and tranquility, so that during the meditation you are neither too slack or too tight, then indeed you are balanced and straight, truly settled in your meditation.

Then on the next occasion it may be that while you are sitting, you try to regulate the body harmoniously, but the Qi breath does not respond to directions. In the case where the Qi breath cannot be regulated, then you must follow the practical directions given above. When the breath is noisy (wind) or uneven (sighing), the breathing is too quick, the body over burdened, you must use the above mentioned methods to regulate yourself. Whenever you use this "Dao" of breathing, notice how finely the breath spins forth, barely perceptible.

Then again the next time you meditate, even though the body and breath are harmonized, the mind sometimes remains either too deep or too shallow, too loose or too tight and doesn't respond. At such a time, if you aspire to awakening, you must use the above methods to regulate yourself suitably while meditating.

There is no "before and after" in regulating these three faculties. Even though they are not regulated (on one occasion), they can be regulated suitably during the next Zen sitting. As for properly harmonizing the body with the breath and heart-mind, there are no other shared vehicles for keeping them together in harmony (than the methods explained above).

If you can blend them together so they are regulated as one harmonious unit, then you can get rid of all your impediments and worries, and keep all obstacles from arising. At last, you (will be able to) master of the way of Zen meditation.

Finally, there are directions for coming out of meditation. "When coming out of Zen, regulate the three activities for being (a normal) human." When coming out of the realm of Zen meditation, you must first of all free the mind from its state of concentration and think about other things. Open the mouth, exhale, and visualize the breath as passing through all of the pores and joints of the body, freely released into the outer world. Then slowly and gently move your body, shoulders, hands, head and neck. Following this (exercise), move the feet and legs, until the muscles are soft and pliant.

Next, use your hands to massage the pores of the skin on the body. Rub the palms of the hands together until they feel warm, and press them gently to the eye lids, and then open them. Only after the heat of the body generated during meditation is dissipated should you try to stand up and freely leave the meditation area.

If you don't follow these rules, even if when sitting you have attained to mastery of the heart, if you leave the meditation too quickly by force, then the refined Dharma way will not yet be gone, but will remain inside your body (i.e., the transition to the coarse way of the outer world not yet completed).

In such a case your head will ache, and the bones and joints will feel rheumatic pains (*feng lau*). In later meditation sessions you will be filled with anxiety and worry. Thus whenever the heart wants to come out of meditation, each time you must pay close attention to the rules for coming out of Zen concentration.

The method for regulating the body, the breath, and the heart-mind (in this case) is to pass from the refined to the coarse state. This process is called "The proper way to enter, abide in and come forth from Zen meditation." As a Gatha hymn puts it:

Proceeding and pausing have their own order,
The coarse and the refined are not to be rivals;
As in the case of a well-trained horse, which
When spurred gallops, when reigned halts.

The Lotus Sutra says:

All the great multitude, all Bodhisattvas
For measureless innumerable millions of Kalpas,
For the sake of the Buddha path,
Perform diligent service with devotion and care[5]
Enter, abide and come forth from meditation well.
For one hundred thousand Kalpas,
Realize great spiritual bonds
By constantly practicing the moral precepts.[6]
How well can they follow the order (for prayer)
Practicing all compassionate Dharma.

---

1. See Inagaki, p. 268, for the definition of Sanmai, Samadhi, as *Ding* (Jpn.: *Jo*), concentration, a mental state of focusing on one object.

2. The Four Great Things to be avoided, as in the following poem, i.e., the body not tranquil, food not taken in measure, not taking joy in seclusion, and a disturbed mind.

3. *Kungfu*, pronounced *Gongfu* means the exercising of various practices which bring about enlightenment, which in the Buddhist tradition could include the chopping of wood, the carrying of water, growing one's own vegetables in a garden, cleaning the temple, begging, walking on pilgrimages and so forth. All of monastic life is a kind of *Gongfu.*

4. The night is divided into 6 watches of 2 hours each. The Buddhist monastic rule suggests that the monk meditates and chants for two hours in the evening, and two hours in the early morning as part of the Zen way of life.

5. Gongyo, diligent service, practice of the Buddha way; the morning and night services of the Buddhist monastic discipline. See Inagaki, p. 77.

6. Bongyo, moral precepts, the strict rules of monastic purity for attaining emancipation; see Inagaki, p. 15.

5. *UPAYA*: THE BEST MEANS

What is meant by the term practicing *Upaya* (Jpn.: *Hoben*, Chn.: *Fangbian*)? There are five kinds of *Upaya*, most skillful means for the practitioner of Zen (Dhyana) meditation. These are: the yearning to practice, determination, recollection, highest wisdom, and keeping the "One mind."

1. If you yearn (to practice Zen) then you must desire to leave the secular world, with all of its intrigues and skewed values. You must desire, i.e., want to practice Zen concentration, and attain wisdom through the Dharma gate.[1] Therefore it is given the name "to will," "to vow." It is also called "to cherish," and "to take delight in." It includes your power to will, to vow or promise, to enjoy, and take delight in all of the profound Dharma gates. Thus it is called "desire" or "yearning (for *Samadhi*)."Thus the Buddha has said:

For all Dharmas, and Compassion,
Yearning is the source.

2. The zealous who practice with diligence, who with firm resolve keep all of the vows and commandments, cast off the five obstacles (greed, anger, languid melancholy, restless denial, skepticism). (To do this) they practice in the late evening and the early morning (first and last night watch).

They meditate assiduously without wasting time, like the person who uses a drill to strike fire, not resting until finally the heat is sufficient. This is what is meant by practicing with determination. Thus did Buddha teach Ananda,[2] saying:

All Buddhas are of One Mind,
Because they practice with constant diligence,
And thus reach the "Sambodhi" other shore.[3]

So much the more do they desire to practice the Dharma of compassion.

3. Recollection or conceptualization means to conceive of all the world as false and worthless, and Zen meditation and wisdom as the most precious of all things. If you can attain to Zen concentration, then you will be able to implement it (highest wisdom, enlightenment), so that nothing attained will be lost, all spiritual skills will be achieved, true enlightenment will be realized.

(You will realize that) by Buddha's way all sentient beings will be saved. This is the most precious of all things, this is what you must "keep in mind."

4. Highest wisdom is such that if you try to measure the value of worldly pleasures against the worth of Zen meditation's highest wisdom, all sense of worldly (great and little) value is lost. Why is this so, you ask? Because the joys of the world are few and the sorrows many, because its pleasures are empty, so false and without fruit, losing them is unimportant.

The joys of Zen meditation and wisdom are above anguish, beyond conceptual judgment,[4] tranquil, serene, broad and far reaching, abiding apart from life and death, always distant from suffering, these are the profound things attained from Zen wisdom. If you understand this, then you know the meaning of highest wisdom.

You the meditator who have come this far, when you cultivate Samatha-vipasyana meditation, in order to use well the teachings explained below, (in heading five), the notion of Samatha-vipasyana, you must quell the heart-mind to attain it. You are led to do this by entering the Dharma path. This is what I call transcendent wisdom.

5. As for the "One mind" (single heart, single mind), if you would have it, distinguish clearly conceptual image from (non-image, non-judgmental) wisdom. See clearly the likelihood of sorrow and evil in the world. If you comprehend well Zen meditation, the quality (merit) of wisdom, its esteem and majesty, at that time you must firmly decide to be single minded (have one heart-mind) to pursue and perfect the practice of Samatha-vipasyana. (Ed. note: these terms are explained in Chapters 6a and 6b below).

The heart-mind becomes like a vajra (thunder-and-lightning bolt).[5] Heavenly spirits, demons, and ways not in accord with the Dharma cannot harm or defile it. It is harmonized so that it is empty and nothing can grasp or hold onto it. In the end it cannot revert to its worldly state. This is the meaning of "The One Mind."

To sum it all up, it is like a person who is on a journey, who first studied the road, and when he saw the way would be hard to pass, determined resolutely to have "One Mind" (mind and heart one) to cross over the road no matter what the obstacle. This is what is called "transcendent wisdom, one mind." Its meaning is as the saying puts it:

Where there's no wisdom there's no Zen.
Where there's no Zen, there's no wisdom.

---

1. Jpn.: *Homon*, Chn.: *Famen*, means the Buddhist Way, or the Dharma path. In the practical order it includes listening to explanations of the Buddhist scriptures. See Inagaki, p. 107.

2. Ananda, one of the first disciples of the Buddha, was famous for listening to all of his discourses, and is said to have been the first compiler of the Buddha's teachings. See Inagaki, p. 7.

3. The Sambodhi refers to the Sanskrit phrase *Anuttara-samyak-Sambodhi*, the highest kind of wisdom attained by the practice of the highest form of emptying

meditation, including Zen practice and chant. The *Prajna-paramita* scriptures, and the short page long *Heart Sutra* teach this doctrine. See Sekiguchi, p. 56, endnote.

4. The Japanese terms *Muro* (Skrt: *Anasrava*, undefiled wisdom) and *Mui* (Skrt: *Asamskrta*, the eternal, un-created or transcendent world) are technical Buddhist terms which were not translated into Confucian or Taoist terms. *Mui* here refers to annihilating worlds or concepts created in the mind. Kenosis or apophasis, to empty the mind of concept and judgment, is indicated here.

5. The word Kongo (Jpn.; "Jingang" in Chn.; Vajra in Sanskrit) is often translated as "adamantine" or "hard as a diamond." The oral and written tradition of both Zen and Tantric Buddhism use the word to mean a bolt of thunder of lightning that purifies and empties mind and heart of all images and desires.

6a. CORRECT PRACTICE

If you would like to learn the correct way to do Samatha-vipasyana (stop-look) Zen meditation, you must from start to finish (of your practice) work toward refining and eliminating mental images.

There are two kinds of Stop-look (Zen) meditation: sitting practice, and, depending on circumstances, practicing Samatha-vipasyana while doing other activities. The first way for those who desire to perfect Samatha-vipasyana meditation is done while sitting. Even though there are those who wish to practice it while doing the "four modes of activity" (*shiigi*: walking, standing, sitting and lying down), and even though one can learn the way of (Stop-look meditation) by all of these means, still sitting is the most effective. You should agree to use sitting first to understand Samatha-vipasyana meditation. By definition there are five different reasons for doing Stop-look meditation: to overcome the coarse perturbed mind of the beginner, to heal the heart-mind from depression and agitation, to stabilize your mind when needed, to refine (empty) your heart-mind; and to balance (internal) Zen concentration with (external) wisdom, during the practice of Samatha-vipasyana.

The first reason is to overcome the coarse and tumultuous mind of the beginner. You who are called practitioners, when you first sit in Zen, since your heart and mind are coarse and troubled, you must first practice samatha, i.e., concentration or "stopping" the heart-mind, in order to master them. If this doesn't work, then you must practice vipasyana "looking." This is why you are told to "to overcome the beginner's coarse and troubled mind, practice `stop' (samatha) and `look' (vipasyana)." Now if you want to understand what "stop" and "look" mean, you realize that they are two different notions. First you must understand how to practice stopping the mind, then practice looking.

1. Samatha means to "stop" mental images and the heart's desires during meditation. There are three kinds of samatha, i.e., stopping and focusing the mind. The first is to bind the mind's focus to a single spot, such as fixing attention on the tip of the nose or the place just below the navel, not allowing the heart-mind to wander from it. Thus the Sutra says:

The bound mind that cannot wander
Is like a monkey chained to a post.

The second kind of samatha controls the mind from wandering after any thoughts that might occur. I.e., it is easy to control the mind when you don't let it gallop away. Thus it is said:

The five sense roots
(eyes, ears, nose, taste, touch)
are all governed by the heart-mind,
So you must guard it (the heart-mind) well.

The above two kinds of samatha are both concerned with the phenomenal (i.e., concepts and impressions within the mind arising from sense contact with the outer noumenal reality). They should not be separated (i.e., focusing and guarding the mind).

The third kind of samatha focuses on the "true essence" (the Tathagata essence, i.e., the "suchness" essence of the Buddha nature). The so-called "letting the mind follow whatever thoughts arise," all of the dharmas (i.e., the whole universe as the object of thought, see Iwano p. 107b), all these things, you must know, are born from direct and conditioned causes, and have no substantial nature of their own. Thus the heart mind does not (actually) hold onto them. If your heart does not really grasp them, then relinquish the wrongly conceived. This is called samatha (stopping concepts). As the sutra puts it:

All the many Dharmas,
Their causes and conditions,
Are empty, without master.
Let heart-mind rest,
In the root source,
Then you will be called
"*Sramana*" (monk or practitioner)!

You, the practitioner, when you begin to learn Zen, will want to perfect the (Buddhas) of the Ten Directions, the Buddha Dharma of the Three Worlds (past, present, future), you will repeatedly pronounce the monk's vows, help all sentient beings to cross over and seek the highest transcendent Way. Your heart must be firm and strong, like the vajra (diamond-thunder bolt), with diligence and fortitude pressing forward, sacrificing even your own life and body, but if you don't attain the goal of enlightenment (through Zen "stop, look" meditation), then in spite of all the Buddha's Dharma (teachings), in the end you will not escape the recycling wheel.

Thereupon, if you desire to sit upright, correctly focusing with single mind on all Dharma, then your object (of thought) will be on the True reality.

What is meant by the term "all Dharma"? It is a contract you make with your heart-mind to understand each and every Dharma. This means that you understand that all good and bad Dharma, all uncategorized Dharma, all worrisome and troubled Dharma, all that exists in the Three Worlds, birthing and dying, all cause and effect Dharma, all of these are caused by the mind. Therefore the *Jujikyo* (*Dasabhumika-sutra*) states:[1]

The Three Worlds have no other Dharma

Except that of perfecting the One Mind.

If you the practitioner realize that the mind has no reality (nature) of its own, then how can any of the Dharma (things mentally conceived) be real? But if all of the Dharmas are unreal, then they are in fact empty and illusory. If you know they are empty and illusory, then they are (also) void and without a master. If void and without a master, then you can't really hold onto them. Relinquish what can't be held on to, (i.e.) relinquish the concept and let the mind rest. If you let go of them and rest your mind, then you will abide tranquilly in the state of *Asamskrta* (non-act, ***wuwei***), which in turn is the basic root of all Dharma.

If one can let the heart rest in the root source (settle the heart in its origins), then it cannot be sullied. The unsullied heart is freed from the fetters of life, death, and karmic deeds[2] If birth, death, and karmic deeds cease, this is the state of Nirvana. Thus the Buddhist Scriptures say:

If you have a mind that doesn't know

And a mind that doesn't see,

That mind conceiving thought is ill,

Then mind with no thought brings Nirvana.

If in fact you can do this, perfect the mind's "True Nature" through cessation, then you will know that humans are meant to attain Nirvana, that which is called "Great Monk's Gateway (practice)." This is how to explain the way of perfecting "True Nature" by cessation. (True nature is empty, realized in mind's cessation).

2. Vipasyana is "looking" or "contemplating" Zen meditation. There are two kinds of vipasyana "Look" meditation. The first is contemplating opposites in order to control them; the second is contemplating the "True."

The first form of vipasyana is to contemplate things opposed to (Nirvana) so as to heal them. If the mind is unsettled when contemplating, focus on immoral, evil desires so as to heal them. Meditation with a compassionate heart-mind heals hatred and anger. All such examples of contemplating to heal are called "healing by contemplating opposites." From this point on you must not discriminate (the value of) any form of judgment (concepts are not to be judged, or predicated with a verb, whether good or bad).[3]

The second form is "True" contemplation. In this form of contemplation one sees all Dharma as manifestations of wisdom and compassion.[4] The Buddhist scriptures relate:

All Dharmas are transitory,
They exist only in the mind.
If you release them and only see the void,
No images are left to conceive.

You the practitioner, when you first sit in Zen meditation, whatever thoughts come to your mind, all the many Dharmas, if no matter what you try, you can't control your mind, and even if you follow the above directions to practice "true nature" concentration and false thoughts still don't cease, then at that time you should "look" at what the mind records, all of the Dharmas, good, bad, or unclassified, whether they belong to the three poisons (greed, sloth, anger).

If you are conceptualizing all sorts of worldly affairs, then you must practice "opposite" contemplation, on whatever thoughts arise in the heart-mind.

If it is an unsettled ("and so forth") mind, sometimes it has lewd thoughts, sometimes it doesn't. If it is a "Non" (*Wu*) mind, non-mind is no-mind, and how can you say then that it exists? If you say that the mind did have existence, this existence must be in the past, present and future. If you say that the mind existed in the past, the past is already gone, so the past mind no longer exists. If you say that the mind will exist in the future, the future has not yet come, how can the mind be now? If you say that the mind exists in the present, the present itself has not yet been mastered, nor has it been grasped. If the mind cannot be held on to (thoughts are ephemeral), how can it be said to exist?

Put in another way, if one says that the mind exists in the present, then one must scrutinize it carefully. When you look at the mind in the present, there is nothing there which can be perceived as object, and thus (of itself) the mind is not perceived, nor can it be grasped (apart from conceived image), and thus it is not of itself existent.

In yet another sense, if one considers (the notion of) birth and annihilation, the mind too must be subject to these phenomena. The heart-mind is either subject to birth and annihilation or it is not. If it is subject to birth and annihilation, then like all flora (grass and trees) which are born and die, so too the heart-mind must do the same. If this is not a phenomenon that applies to the heart-mind, then how can one attain to that whereby it is born or annihilated?

You must know that the heart-mind cannot be grasped as an object; this is because it does not exist (of itself). In yet another sense, if you say that there is a cause of the present, that in a *ksana* fraction of a second it is born and annihilated, becoming a heart-mind, if we now closely examine it, we see that it still cannot be grasped (in itself), then how can it have "become" a mind?[5]

If you say that it is born and annihilated in the present, then it must be that the past mind died and the present mind is born, or else you must hold that it did not die in the past but is born (now). But if you say that the heart-mind of the past did not die, and the heart-mind of the present is just now born, from whence is it born? If it did not die and is born, then there must be two heart-minds existant (one giving birth to the other). Otherwise, how can it be said that the mind does not die and is born?

If it is born from that which does not die, or if it is not born from that which does not die, either way the non-existent or the existent is birthed. If the non-existent is born, then the non-existent dies; but if the non-existent is born and dies (in the process of thinking and willing), how can you arrive at the conclusion that it "becomes" a mind? Thus you must realize that the heart-mind cannot be grasped or held onto (as if it "became" a thing).

Again one can say that in the process of Zen concentration there is a heart-mind operating in the present; if so, one can ask whether the heart is born of itself, of another, of itself and another, or not of itself and another. If you say that it is born of itself, then if there is no external object present then there is no mind existent, and thus it cannot be born of itself.

If you say it is born from another, if that other Dharma (thing) is a mind, then there must be another mind from which that mind is born; you cannot say that the mind of another is one's own mind. If the other thing is not a mind, how can that which is not a mind give birth to a mind? If you say that self and other together are the cause of heart-mind's birth, this too is impossible. If the self and the other both have a heart-mind, then there is no need to wait until the two are united for the mind to be born.

If the heart mind does not exist in the self or the other, then when united it cannot be born either. If you say that it is born neither from the self or the other, then it must be born from the empty void. But in fact this is impossible, because as said above, (the mind) born from conditioned causes cannot be grasped (held on to, obtained). How can it be born from non-cause?

Thus for all the above causes and reasons, we are forced to admit that what is born in the mind in the end cannot be grasped as external reality.

If what the mind looks at in itself cannot be grasped, so much the more is it impossible to grasp what is seen as wisdom. If it is impossible to grasp whatever can be, or is seen by the heart-mind. Thus "All that is Mind" (the One Mind) cannot be attained. If the One Mind cannot be grasped, then All of the Dharma cannot be attained. If All Dharma cannot be grasped, then the heart-mind is not reliable.

If the heart-mind is not reliable, there is nothing to think about. If there's nothing to think about, then all is reversed, thinking itself is cut-off. If all is turned around and thinking is cut off, then the mind no longer discriminates (i.e., makes no discriminatory judgments). If the heart-mind no longer discriminates, then the argumentative disputing mind rests, and there are no more feelings of love and hate. When coarse and fine contemplation (Skrt: *vitarka, vicara*), i.e., simple or complex thoughts do not arise, then the body and mind are at peace.

When body and mind are at peace, only then can you attain true Zen concentration. With true Zen concentration comes forth a Tathagata's true wisdom and compassion, all birthing and annihilation are left behind. Thus a hymn from the Buddha's discourses states:

The Prajna-paramita (shore of wisdom)
Is a true Dharma, not a false, inverted one,
Concept, image, contemplation are all obstacles,
The Dharma of words are all obliterated.
Immeasurable transgressions annihilate as obstacles,
The pure peaceful heart is always "one."
If thus you respect the Wondrous One (Buddha)
You will see the shore of Prajna wisdom.

The above is by way of explaining how the beginner can break through the heart-mind's confusion and practice Samatha-vipasyana "stop, look" meditation.

The second reason to practice "stop, look" meditation (as stated in the beginning) is to heal the illness of depression and over elation in the heart-mind of the meditator. You, the practitioner, when you wish to practice Zen sitting, and your mind is dark and inhibited, and you cannot remember or recall what to do, or are drowsy, then you must at this point practice vipasyana "looking" contemplation. If while you are sitting your heart-mind is "floating" (over-excited or elated), flitting about lightly and restless, at that time you must practice samatha concentration to stop it. This is how one uses Samatha-vipasyana to heal the phenomena of the heat-mind's depression and hyperaction. "You must know well the best medicine to heal illness according to the directives. If you don't follow the directives one-by-one, you will have false results and lose the effectiveness (of Zen meditation)."

The third reason to learn Stop-Look meditation is so that you may practice Zen continuously, in the manner that it is most convenient to do so. To do this you, the practitioner must, when sitting in Zen meditation, learn how to curb the heart-mind's sinking (into depression or sleep) by practicing vipasyana "looking."

But if the heart-mind is not bright and clear (when doing vipasyana), and there is no way to gain any profit from meditating in this manner, then you must know when to use samatha concentration to control it. That is, if when you are practicing samatha cessation (of mind's judgments and will's desires) and you feel that the body and the heart-mind are peaceful and tranquil in so doing, then you must realize that it is easier to practice samatha "Stop" meditation at such a time, and so you can use samatha to quiet the heart-mind.

But if you the practitioner when sitting in Zen meditation try to use samatha "Stop" techniques to heal the giddy and distracted mind, and the heart-mind does not respond, and there is no longer any profit to be gained from this method, then you must realize that it is time to practice vipasyana "look" contemplation.

If while practicing vipasyana you achieve peace and tranquility of heart and spirit, finding contentment in solitude and tranquility, then know that it is now best to practice "Look" contemplation. Thus is it said that one must practice samatha or vipasyana according to what is most convenient and useful.

You must agree to practice only what is good,
Things which are beneficial for you to do;
Thus that which makes heart and spirit tranquil,
Quells the mind of troublesome worries,
Are what confirm the Dharma path.

The fourth reason to practice "Stop," "Look" meditation is to refine the heart mind while perfecting Samadhi concentration. You, the practitioner, must know that you first use "Stop," "Look" Samatha Vipasyana to break away from the disturbed, confused mind. Once the disturbed mind is quieted, then you will be able to enter into Samadhi's focused concentration. Because you have refined the mind to a state of Samadhi concentration, you will feel that the body is empty and secluded, and will take great joy in this.

If you benefit from this change,
Arising from within the heart-mind,
Then you can use the refined heart
As reason to dispel the mind's evil deceit.

If you do not control the mind so as to realize its falseness, then avarice will of necessity arise. "Avarice arises when the mind takes its concepts to be real." If you know that mental images are false and not real, then attraction to sense images will not arise. This is what is called practicing Samatha or "stopping images."

But if you repeatedly practice Samatha "stop" meditation, and the heart-mind is still enticed and distracted, "The desire to see cannot be controlled or arrested," then at that time you must practice Vipasyana "look" meditation, and while looking refine the heart-mind, i.e., if you don't experience a control and refining of the mind while doing Samatha.

Seeing that you don't succeed in controlling
The mind from images seen while doing Samatha,
And exotic visions disturb and stain your mind,
Then choose Vipasyana looking to destroy all visions.

This is called Vipasyana or "look" practice. All of the above is by way of explaining through examples how to handle and control the refining of the heart-mind when doing Zen meditation, by practing in turn Samatha-Vipasyana "Stop, Look" reflection.

The method of distinguishing Stop and Look
Is explained in the above passages.
If you don't succeed by "stopping" the image,
Use the other way, "Looking" to destroy it.

The fifth reason to practice "Stop" "Look" Zen is to perfect true wisdom. If you the practitioner while sitting in Zen meditation, because of practicing either "Stop" or "Look" enter into a state of Zen Samadhi (awakened stillness), even though you have entered into Samadhi, it does not follow that you have envisioned true wisdom. If you have not conceived true wisdom, your Zen is diseased; you have not cut off attachment.

Indeed your vision of wisdom is tenuous and fragile
True wisdom cannot yet arise,
To let you cut off all attachments,
And enter all the Dharma gates!

At such a time you must practice Vipasyana "Looking" (at the mental images) to cut off attachment and discrimination. If while in the state of samatha concentration wisdom begins too arise, i.e., "Samadhi awakening and wisdom are in balance," then you will be able to use it (wisdom) to cut off attachments, "the proof of all Dharma gates."

But if you the practitioner, when sitting in Zen meditation, whether doing "Stop" or "Look" contemplation, have not yet quieted your heart mind, wisdom is onerous ("too much," i.e., not tempered by compassion which arises from "Looking outward"). Then the heart-mind is suddenly uncontrolled, wisdom loses its radiance, and "focused mind is not achieved," because focus is insufficient, and the heart-mind is restless and scattered. It is like the flame of a lantern flickering in the wind, not emitting enough light to shine on things. Thus Buddha's discourse states:

If you haven't focused the heart-mind,
Even if your wisdom contemplates the
"Void, no image," and so forth.,
This is an upside-down wisdom,

A mad wisdom;

You cannot escape from the life-death cycle.

At such a time you must return to the practice of "Stop" (Samatha) meditation, because by practicing samatha you can focus and calm the heart-mind. A focused and calm heart mind is like a lamp that is in a hidden room, which can pierce the darkness and shed light on things with widespread radiance. The foregoing is by way of explaining how to perfect equally the mind's focus and wisdom by practicing "Stop" and "Look" meditation.

You the practitioner, if you are able to do as stated above, can while the body is in the correct sitting position, use these five means to judge when to do Samatha "Stop" and Vipasyana "Look" with images arising during meditation, choosing one or the other without losing the benefits of either one. You must know that this is how you and I can practice the Buddha's Dharma teaching in a compassionate manner; we must not pass through our whole life in an empty barren way.

---

1. The (Chn.) *Shidi Jing* (Jpn. *Juji-kyo*) is the first chapter of the greater Hua Yen Ching, the *Avatamsaka-sutra*. In it the ten stages of a Bodhisattva's enlightenment are explained. See Iwano (1965) p. 149a.

2. A karmic deed here means an action done as the result of mental imaging and heart willing a given object. Actions stemming from the animal or vegetable functions such as nutrition and rest needs are not karmic, i.e., without retribution.

3. This point, non-discriminatory image, is best exemplified in the Tibetan Tankha paintings of the Yag-yum, male and female figures embracing. The symbol represents the union of compassion (male) with wisdom (female). The foreigner or novice who approaches the master with the discriminatory mind (judging the Tanka symbol to have sexual meaning) is rejected as a disciple of Tantric meditation.

4. As in Endnote 3, above; compassion without wisdom is a violent male spirit. Wisdom without compassion is a female demon. Tantric art depicts the brains, heart, eyes, and intestines being pulled out of the meditator as a graphic way of describing the need to eliminate all images from the heart-mind before transcendent union. The sacred *Cham* dances of Labrang, and other Tibetan monasteries end in a great fire rite wherein all obstacles are burned away.

5. I.e., the idea conceived in the mind is not the thing, nor does the mind "become" the thing each time that it conceives a thought, then cease to be when the act of thinking ends. The mind itself is not an object that can be grasped by the senses, i.e., itself is not a thing that is perceived, born, or dies. (Ed. note).

6b. OTHER WAYS TO DO ZEN

Understand, you who practice "Stop" "Look" Zen, that we must face conditional causes when we encounter the external world outside of meditation. Though sitting in the upright position is the very best way to perfect your body, there are innumerable occasions when you must get bodily involved in the things and conditions of the worldly. If you have not practiced and perfected "Stop" "Look" (Samatha Vipasyana), then the opportunities to improve your-heart-mind will be limited to meditation.

Attachment to karmic deeds will arise as you encounter external things. How can you hasten to respond to them in the Buddhist way? If you can at all times, with constancy practice the *upaya* skills of samadhi concentration and wisdom, you must be aware that by so doing, you can attain to all of the Buddha's teachings (Dharma).

What does it mean to practice "Stop" "Look" Zen while passing through worldly causes and conditions? There are six conditions *(pratitya)* in which you can practice: walking, standing, sitting, lying down (resting), doing work, and talking.

What is meant by "practicing Samatha Stopping and Vipasyana looking according to external circumstances?" There are six kinds of worldly circumstances: the eyes look at colors (sensual attraction); the ears hear sound; the nose smells; the tongue tastes; the body feels by touch; and the mind conceptualizes images (Dharma). You the practitioner can perfect "Stop" "Look" meditation in all twelve of these external circumstances. Thus is it called "Perfecting Samatha Vipasyana while encountering the external world."

As for the first, "walking" or going somewhere, while walking there you should think about "for what reason do I want to go to there and what desire (*klesa*) moves me?" If the reason is not done out of compassion and the affair itself is of no account, then there is no need to go. If the motive is compassion and there is more than ordinary benefit to going, and it is a deed in keeping with the Buddhist way (Dharma), then you should go. What is the meaning of "practicing Samatha ("stop" meditation) while walking?"

If while walking you put an end to all judgmental thoughts, and due to (centering on) the act of walking itself, of all the good and evil thoughts that arise, there isn't one that you focus on, with the result that delusory thoughts do not arise, this is called practicing Samatha while walking.

What does it mean to practice Vipasyana (Look meditation) while walking? To do this you must when walking think about the fact that the will causes the body to move, and that going out and coming back are due to this (the mind's judgment and will's desire). Therefore all good and bad Dharma (thoughts) that arise, are called "karmic deeds." [1]

You must now reflect inwardly on the heart mind, while walking. Inside the heart mind itself there are no images or appearances to be seen. You the walking person must now be aware that all Dharmas (concepts envisioned in the mind) are in the long run empty and isolated from reality. This is what is called practicing Vipasyana looking while walking. Thus while walking you can practice Samatha Vipasyana "Stop" "Look" meditation as was described above.

Second, it is possible to practice "Stop" "Look" meditation while standing or staying in some place. To do this you must ask yourself when staying in some place "why am I staying here and to fulfill what purpose do I desire to be here?" If it is not a compassionate deed or a thing worth noting, then you should not stay there. But if you do a deed out of compassion with extraordinary benefit, then you should stay.

Why is this called practicing Samatha "Stop" meditation while staying somewhere? If while you are staying there you cut off all judgmental thoughts, knowing that due to staying there all sorts of good and bad Dharma thoughts will arise, but due to not holding on to these images not one of them will give rise to false or illusory thoughts, then such a practice is called "Samatha" (stopping images and judgments).

How does one practice Vipasyana (Look" meditation while staying somewhere? While doing this deed (stopping somewhere) you should think that it is due to the mind and will that movement is controlled and managed, making the body stop and stay somewhere. Due to this all sorts of good and bad Dharma images will arise, due to your "staying."

Now look at your heart-mind, as it is staying here. The heart-mind is of itself without form or image. You must realize that all Dharma images that arise in the mind are also in the final count empty and isolated from reality. This is "practicing Vipasyana looking." You can also practice wisdom meditation was explained above in "walking."

Third, it is possible to practice "Stop" "Look" meditation while sitting in some place. To do this you must ask yourself when sitting in some place "why am I sitting here and to fulfill what purpose do I desire to be here?" If it is not a compassionate deed or a thing worth noting, then you should not sit there. But if you do a deed out of compassion with extraordinary benefit, then you should sit there.

Why is this called practicing Samatha "Stop" meditation while sitting? If while you are sitting there you cut off all judgmental thoughts, knowing that due to sitting all sorts of good and bad Dharma thoughts will arise, but due to not holding on to these images not one of them will give rise to false or illusory thoughts, then such a practice is called "Samatha" (stopping images and judgments while sitting).

How does one practice Vipasyana "Look" meditation while sitting? While doing this deed (sitting) you should think that it is due to the mind and will that sitting here you can rest the feet and quiet the body. Due to this all sorts of good and bad Dharma images will arise, due to your "sitting." Now look at your heart-mind as you are sitting here. The heart-mind is of itself without form or image. You must realize that all Dharma images that arise in the mind are also in the final count empty and isolated from reality. This is "practicing Vipasyana looking." Thus, you can practice wisdom meditation while sitting, as explained above.

Fourth, it is possible to practice "Stop" "Look" meditation while lying down. To do this you must ask yourself when lying down "why am I resting here and to what purpose do I desire to be here?" If doing it is not according to Buddhist practice (Dharma), or due to laziness, then you should not be resting.

But if it is done in order to regulate the "Four Great" things (the four elements, and the four needs of the body, nourishment, warmth, exercise, rest), then you should rest. When resting, you should lie down as the Lion King did.[2] (Rest only when needed, wherever a resting place can be found).

What is meant by practicing Samatha "Stop" meditation while resting? If while you are resting you cut off all judgmental thoughts, knowing that due to resting there all sorts of good and bad

Dharma thoughts will arise, but due to not holding on to these images not one of them will give rise to false or illusory thoughts, then such a practice is called "Samatha" (stopping images and judgments while resting).

How does one practice Vipasyana "Look" meditation while resting? While doing this deed (resting) you should consider that when the heart-mind has become tired, you must allow it to rest, and fall asleep, letting go control of the six senses. Due to this all sorts of good and evil Dharma arise, during the time that you are resting.

Now reflect on your heart-mind as you are reclining. Looking at the heart-mind, it is without form or image of itself. You must realize that while sleeping all Dharma images that arise in the mind are in the final count empty and isolated from reality. This is "practicing Vipasyana looking." You can also practice wisdom meditation while resting, as was explained above under "walking."

Fifth, it is possible to practice "Stop" "Look" meditation while working or doing something. To do this you must ask yourself when working "why am I doing this and to fulfill what purpose do I desire to do it?" If it is not a compassionate deed or a thing worth noting, then you should not do it. But if you are doing it out of compassion with extraordinary benefit, then you should do it. Why is this called practicing Samatha "Stop" meditation while working? If while you are working you cut off all judgmental thoughts, knowing that due to working all sorts of good and bad Dharma thoughts will arise, but due to not holding on to these images not one of them will give rise to false or illusory thoughts, then such a practice is called "Samatha" (stopping images and judgments while working).

How does one practice Vipasyana "Look" meditation while working? While doing this deed you should think that it is due to the mind and will that the body and the hands move while you are doing this and all sorts of work. Due to the heart-mind all sorts of good and bad Dharma images will arise, due to your "working."

Now reflect on your heart-mind as you are working. You do not see any form or image in the heart-mind itself. You must realize that all Dharma images that arise in the mind are also in the final count empty and isolated from reality. This is "practicing Vipasyana looking." You can also practice wisdom meditation while working, as was explained above under the title of "walking."

Sixth, it is possible to practice "Stop" "Look" meditation while talking. To do this you must ask yourself when talking "why am I doing this and to fulfill what purpose do I desire to discuss it?" If you are not compassionate or your words worth noting, then you should not speak. But if you are talking out of compassion with extraordinary benefit, then you should speak.

Why is this called practicing Samatha "Stop" meditation while talking? If while you are talking you realize that all sorts of good and bad Dharma thoughts will arise, but due to not holding on to these images not one of them will give rise to false or illusory thoughts, then such a practice is called "Samatha" (stopping all Dharma images and judgments while talking).

How does one practice Vipasyana "Look" meditation while talking? While speaking you must think how it is due to the mind and will that awakening occurs through Vipasyana looking. The heart-mind stirs and moves the Qi breath, the beats of inhaling and exhaling propel the lips, teeth, tongue and gums, putting out sounds that form words. Because of this action, all sorts of good and bad Dharma images will arise, due to your "talking."

Now reflect on your heart-mind as you are speaking. You do not see any form or image in the heart-mind itself. You must realize that all Dharma images that arise in the mind are also in the final count empty and isolated from reality. This is "practicing Vipasyana talking." You can also practice wisdom meditation while talking, as was explained above under "walking."

Seventh, how can you practice "Stop" "Look" meditation while the eyes see color? While looking at colors (the object of vision) you must know that color is like the moon reflected in water, there is no steady or defined shape. If you see a color that is pleasant, don't let feelings of attraction arise; if you see a color that is unpleasant, don't let feelings of repulsion occur. If you see something that is neither pleasant or unpleasant, don't let *avidya* (Chn: *Wuming*, ignorance of the four noble truths) i.e., lack of compassion arise,[3] or any confused, disorderly thoughts disturb your mind; this is called Samatha "Stop" practice.

How practice Vipasyana "Look" meditation while looking at sense objects or color? You must think while looking that even though there is the act of seeing, that which defines the act of seeing, i.e. the mental image, does not exist (as a thing). Now if we ask why this is so, this act of seeing (as with the all of the five senses) is rooted in the particles of the external world. Neither the void space between the external world, the five senses or the act of *ming* knowledge are seen, or differentiated in the act of seeing. But by the joining of cause and condition, the act of the eyes seeing and mind knowing are born or produced.

The eyes and the mind are cause and condition for giving birth to the intellect's knowing. When the intellect is produced or born, only then can the mind differentiate or judge the many kinds of sense images and colors. They exist because of this process. All good, bad and indifferent Dharma must then be reflected on by Vipasyana "looking," seeing that the mind which conceives color or sense images in fact is not seeing them as they really are, i.e., mental images are not real, don't exist.

You must realize that the act of seeing itself as well as all kinds of Dharma (images) are in the end result empty and isolated from reality. This is called Vipasyana, "Looking." You can also practice "Stop" "Look" meditation while seeing color or sense images, distinguishing which is more beneficial, as was explained above.

Eighth, you can practice "Stop" "Look" meditation while the ears are hearing sound. As the sound is heard, you must know that sound itself is but a concept formed from noise. If you hear a sound that is smooth and pleasant, don't let your heart be attached to it; if you hear a sound that is unpleasant, don't let your feelings dislike it; if the sound is neither harsh or pleasant, don't let the mind judge it. This is called practicing Samatha "Stop" meditation through sound.

How practice Vipasyana "Looking" with sound? You must while listening do as follows. Realize that whatever sound you hear is empty of itself, there is nothing which exists of itself. But by joining yourself to the particles of the external world, the act of hearing and knowing are born from the ears and the mind. The ears and mind are causes, and that which is produced is hearing and knowing. From this arises a strong sense of discriminatory judgment. From this it follows that all good, bad and indifferent Dharma arise from this act called hearing.

Now if you reflect on the mind by using Vipasyana "Look" meditation, you will not see the image or the form of sound there. From this you must realize that the act of listening and all kinds of Dharma (concepts) are in the final count empty and isolated from reality. This is called Vipasyana, "Looking" at or contemplating sound. You can also practice "Stop" "Look" meditation while listening to sound for wisdom, as was explained above.

Ninth, you can practice "Stop" "Look" meditation while the nose is smelling scent. As the scent is smelled, you must know that scent itself changeable, is unreal. If you smell a fragrance that is smooth and pleasant, don't let your heart be attached to it. If you smell an odor that is unpleasant, don't let your feelings dislike it. If the smell is neither harsh or pleasant, don't let the mind be disturbed by it. This is called practicing Samatha "Stop" meditation through scent.

How practice Vipasyana "Looking" with scent? You must while smelling do as follows. Realize that whatever scent you smell is empty of itself, there is nothing which exists of itself. But by joining yourself to the particles of the external world, the nose and mind give birth, producing a sense and knowledge of smell, forcing a strong sense image of fragrance. Good, bad and indifferent Dharma arise, due to what is called smelling fragrance.

Now if you reflect on the mind by using Vipasyana "Look" meditation, you will not see the image or the form of smell there. From this you must realize that from the act of smelling all kinds of Dharma (concepts) arise, which are in the final count empty and isolated from reality. This is called Vipasyana, "Looking" at or contemplating smell. You can also practice "Stop" "Look" meditation while smelling, to gain wisdom, as was explained above.

Tenth, you can practice "Stop" "Look" meditation while the tongue is tasting flavor. As the flavor is tasted, you must realize that flavor is like something tasted in a dream. If you taste something that is smooth and pleasant, don't let your heart be attached to it. If you taste something that is unpleasant, don't let your feelings dislike it. If the taste is neither harsh or pleasant, don't let the mind be judgmental or discriminatory about it. This is called practicing Samatha "Stop" meditation through taste.

How practice Vipasyana "Looking" through taste? You must while the tongue tastes something do as follows. Realize that whatever flavor you taste cannot of itself be held onto, there is no flavor which exists of itself. This is why the inner six tastes and outer six flavors[4] cannot by their own nature be discriminated. They depend on the tongue of the taster to be judged. The tongue, in its roots, does not have knowledge. Only when tongue and mind are joined, are knowledge and judgment born, forcing a strong sense image of taste. Due to taste, good, bad and indifferent Dharma arise.

Now if you reflect on the mind by using Vipasyana "Look" meditation, you will not see the image or the form of taste there. From this you must realize that from the act of tasting all kinds of Dharma (concepts) arise, which are in the final count empty and isolated from reality. This is called Vipasyana, "Looking" at or contemplating taste. You can also practice "Stop" "Look" meditation while tasting, to gain wisdom, as was explained above.

Eleventh, you can practice Samatha "Stop" meditation while the body experiences the sense of touch. Thus while feeling the sensation of touch, you must realize that it is unreal like a changing dream. If the sensation is pleasant, don't become attached to it. If unpleasant or painful, don't let feelings of repulsion arise. If indifferent, don't allow the intellect to pass judgment on it. This is what we call practicing Samatha "Stop" meditation while experiencing the sense of touch.

How can you practice "Look" Vipasyana while the body senses touch? You must at such a time ponder that sensations such as cold and warm, rough and smooth, light and heavy are all called touch sensations felt by the head, body and its four limbs, joining it to the external four elements (earth, water, fire, wind).[5] The body's sensations are by nature empty and void, and the body itself is not real (i.e., co-dependent on all other being for its existence).

Whenever anyone experiences the sense of touch, thus joined to the (external world of) causal conditions, first knowledge of the body is born, followed by the birth of cognition, the judgmental mind, and all images such as sorrow and joy, etc. This is what we call the sensation of touch, which you should now reflect upon, seeing that the heart mind joined to external causal conditioning does not in fact perceive that is but a conceptual form and image that is seen.

You must realize that to admit touch sensation or any other form of Dharma mental concept is in the long run no more than an empty experience, isolated from reality. This is called "Looking" or contemplating the sense of touch. While experiencing the sense of touch you can also prepare to practice "Stop" "Look" for compassionate wisdom, as described above.

Twelfth, the mind while thinking can practice "Stop" "Look" meditation by contemplating mental concepts. This kind of practice was explained at the beginning of Chapter 6a, controlling the beginner's mind as an introduction to Zen meditation. It need not be repeated here.

If you the meditator are able to practice Samatha "Stop" and Vipasyana "Look" while walking, standing, sitting and reclining, while seeing, hearing, feeling and knowing, i.e., in all circumstances, you must realize that you are practicing the true Mahayana way, (the shore of wisdom and compassion). As is said in the Great Prajnaparamita sutra:

The Buddha spoke to Subhuti,[6] saying

"If a Bodhisattva while walking perceives walking,

While sitting observes sitting, And so on...,
While dressed in the robes of a monk finds profit
Keeping focused solely on the `one' heart-mind,
When entering into and coming out of Zen meditation.
You must realize that this is called
The Bodhisattva's way of Mahayana practice,
That no (Dharma, mental image) can be kept.

To summarize, if you do as explained above, practicing the Mahayana way (of wisdom and compassion through "Stop" "Look" meditation) in all circumstances, this will allow you while in the world to be the most excellent, unsurpassed practitioner without equal. It is as the Buddha said in the Gatha hymn:

While sitting alone amidst the trees in a forest,
Heart-mind floating freely without cares or worries,
Such joy surpasses even heaven's bliss.
All the profit that humans seek,
Fame, fancy clothes, house and trappings,
Are transient pleasures, without inner peace,
Oppressive craving for profit never satisfied.
Don the monk's robes, go begging for food,
When moving or resting,
The heart-mind is always "one."[7]
If from within you always use your eye of wisdom,
"Looking" at mind, all Dharmas, and reality,
Then you can handle all kinds of Dharma images,
Looking on all of them, completely impartial,
The heart-mind liberated, by wisdom,
Into peaceful solitude.
Nothing in the Three Worlds (past, present, future)
Can compare to this!

1. A pun on the word *xing* for walking, which is also used for "Karmic deeds." N.B., *karma* means deeds, not fate.

2. The Lion King, Simha, 24th of the 28 Zen patriarchs of India. Famous for teaching Dhyana meditation, he slept only as was needed, for the sake of maintaining health.

3. *Avidya* or *Wuming* refers here to a lack of understanding of the Four Noble Truths, the basic teaching of Buddhism, i.e., all life is conditioned by suffering, suffering is caused by selfish desire, annihilate selfishness, and follow the way of compassion (i.e. the eight fold path to enlightenment).

4. Sweet, sour, hot, mild, salty, bland.

5. The *liu fen* six divisions of the body are the head, trunk, arms, and legs; the "four great elements" are earth, for body's strength, water for refreshing and containing, fire for warming and wind for movement and growth. See Inagaki 1985:., p. 291.).

6. Subhuti was said to have been the sixteenth disciple of the Buddha, to whom the doctrine of *Sunya* emptiness was preached. See Sekiguchi: 1992, p. 86.

7. I.e., focused in Samatha Vipasyana "Stop" "Look" mode.

7. ROOTS OF COMPASSION

Today we shall explain the manifestation of good, compassionate roots which were sown in the preceding chapters. There are two kinds of compassionate roots, outer and inner.

The first kind, compassionate roots manifested in the exterior world, include works of compassionate giving (*dana*), keeping the rules of the monks, love of parents and respect to people with authority over me, making offerings to the Three Treasures (Buddha, his Dharma teachings, and the Sangha community of followers), reading, chanting, hearing and learning the Buddhist scriptures. In all of these things the roots of compassion are goodness are manifest, but they can be corrupted by ideas and images from the demonic realm, as will be discussed later.

The second kind of good roots manifested are those of the internal order, i.e., all of the Zen Dharma methods, where good roots first sprout forth. There are three such manifestations: a true understanding of the concept of compassionate roots budding; the ability to distinguish true from false roots; and understanding how to use "Stop" and "Look" meditation continuously to nourish these good roots.

1. The Budding of Compassionate Roots.

What is the meaning of "Sprouting good roots internally?" There are five kinds of good roots, the sprouting of each one different from the other. The first is to stabilize breathing. The second is to contemplate the unclean; the third is compassion blossoming; the fourth is the contemplation of the twelve causal conditions (*Nidanas*); the fifth is the visualization of the Buddha's image.

First, let us speak of how the way of breathing sprouts good roots. You the practitioner, due to perfecting the practice of Samatha "Stop" and Vipasyana "Look" meditation, will regulate and harmonize body and mind, spurious images will not arise, and you will feel from within your heart-mind that you have gradually entered into a state of meditative concentration.

This feeling, however, arises while you are still in the realm of desire,[1] as also in the condition just before reaching the level of *Samadhi*, "concentrating on a single object."[2] The body and heart-mind gradually become empty and isolated. The heart-mind when in *Samadhi* is still and quiescent, and while in this condition no longer sees the body or mind's form or shape.

After experiencing this, whether in one or two sittings, days or months, you will find that the control of the breath is also mastered, so that it is neither constrained or insufficient. When this happens, while in the state of *Samadhi* you will be able to sense even the lightest movements of body and heart-mind, and the eight sense impressions will be enhanced.

What are these eight sense impressions? They are (as explained in Chapter 6a) the body's slightest awareness of movement, itching, cold, warmth, lightness, heaviness, roughness and smoothness. When these sensations occur the body and heart-mind are at last stilled. You will find delight in this subtle, refined emptiness, take joy in quiet stillness, something to be experienced, not explained. This is the source and end result of counting in and out breathing, an excellent source for producing Zen *Samadhi.*

Another way for you, the Zen practitioner, to do this, whether in the desire realm or the form world, before entering true Samadhi meditation, is to note the exhaling and inhaling of breath, whether long or short, feel the pores on the entire body and the hands to be open and unobstructed (i.e., feel yourself to breathe in and out through the pores of the body).

Also, you can use the mind's eye to look at (breath passing through) the interior of the body with its 36 stages,[3] like a great warehouse that is opened, in which you see hemp, grain, seeds and beans; the heart-mind is amazed and delighted with the sight, enthralled with the solitude, stillness and peace therein. Such is the result of contemplating the exhaling and inhaling of breath (and its passage through the body), and the (sixteen) internal masteries due to regulated breathing,[4] which bring about the sprouting of compassionate roots within.

Second, good roots can be manifest in contemplating things that are unclean. You the practitioner, if you are still in the desire or form world, i.e., not yet in the state of true *Samadhi,* with body and mind as empty and isolated, suddenly see the bodies of men and women as dead, corpses already excreting pus and rotting, worms crawling in and out, white bones lying scattered about; then let your heart be filled with sorrow and joy, that the things you used to love are now oppressive and harmful. This is to make good roots sprout forth by using the nine images.[5]

Or, if you are a beginner at Zen meditation,[6] when you first sit, see suddenly the inner and outer parts of your own body as unclean; see the bowls and guts lying all scattered about, ones own body as white bleached bones, from the top of the head to the tip of the toes. Visualize every joint in the body and fix the gaze on them, seeing the above conditions to be already in effect.[7]

Then your heart-mind will experience *Samadhi's* peace and stillness; suddenly awakened to the fact that nothing is constant! The oppressive harm of the five desires[8] no longer effects me! This is to make manifest the good roots of "letting go," or liberation.[9]

Or you may also visualize your body, inside and out, all birds that fly and animals that move, clothes and food, houses, forests and hills, all to be unclean or sullied. This making of all things great and small unclean is a manifestation of good roots sprouting.

Third, good roots bring forth a compassionate heart-mind. When you the practitioner, due to practicing Samatha "Stop" and Vipasyana "Look" meditation, have mastered the world of desires but not yet attained to the realm of *Samadhi* (i.e., still in the world of forms), while you are doing your Zen meditation, you will suddenly see arising in your mind images of compassion towards all sentient beings, or gratitude to your family, and due to this (compassionate heart) you will take great joy in these images.

There upon you will enter a deeper stage of Zen *Samadhi*, the inner heart-mind purified and cleansed, and an indescribable peace and joy will be yours. You will also feel compassion towards strangers, enemies, a compassion that extends everywhere in the ten directions and all sentient beings in the five realms (deva, human, preta, demon, asura). If you continue to practice this meditation, no matter whom you meet, your facial expression will always be tranquil and harmonious. This is called the compassionate heart sprouting from good roots.

Other good roots such as the three immeasurables, kindness, joy, and renunciation or detachment are also manifest in the same way as compassion, as described above.

Fourth, good roots are manifest by contemplating the (twelve) Nidanas,[10] "causal conditions" that keep you from enlightenment. When you the practitioner, due to practicing Samatha "Stop" and Vipasyana "Look" meditation, have mastered the world of desires but not yet attained to the realm of *Samadhi* (i.e., still in the world of forms), while you are doing your Zen meditation you will suddenly experience the beginning or birth of enlightenment in your heart-mind.

Then contemplate the Three Worlds (past, present, future), how so much *klesa* ignorance (the second Nidana) and selfish karmic deeds occur, and while absorbed in contemplating the Twelve Nidanas, you no longer see others or your self, then you will be able to leave the desire for short life or long life, break through all evil desires, and attain the state of *Samadhi's* steady internal peace.

You will be liberated, awakened to wisdom and its manifestations; in your heart will be born joy in the Dharma. You will no longer think about the things of the world, nor the five *Skhandas*[11] and the twelve accesses to the mind,[12] and the eighteen realms of perception arising from these,[13] as well as subsequent distinctions and judgments. This is what we call the sprouting of good roots from contemplating the Twelve Nidanas.

Fifth, good roots are manifest by contemplating Buddhist images. When you the practitioner, due to practicing Samatha "Stop" and Vipasyana "Look" meditation, have mastered the world of desires but not yet attained to the realm of *Samadhi* (i.e., still in the world of forms), while you are doing your Zen meditation when body and heart mind are in *Sunya* void solitude, you will suddenly be flooded with images in which the multitude of the Buddhas will appear as filling you with their good merit, more than can be imagined, given to me by their merit.

These include: the ten powers,[14] the four kinds of fearlessness,[15] the (eighteen) uncommon powers,[16] *Samadhi* (heart-mind void, without images or karmic deeds), and the 108 forms of liberation.[17] You cannot begin to imagine the number of spiritual transformations, explaining the Dharma without obstacle, broad benefits for all sentient beings, due to their immeasurable merits.

While you are contemplating these images, feelings of respectful love will be born in your heart, *Samadhi* will be awakened, body and heart mind filled with elation, pure and tranquil. No evil thoughts will occur, from the time that Zen *Samadhi* awakens. The body will feel light and blessed, and from within you will feel that the Buddha's merit towers above you. This respectful love has sprouted forth from the good root of visualizing the Buddha's *Samadhi*.

Besides the above, you the practitioner, due to perfecting "Stop" "Look" meditation, will attain to purity and tranquility of body and heart-mind, all of the Dharma gates will be open and manifest to you, including realizing that everything is impermanent and brings suffering, that there is no self, no purity. The affairs of the world are oppressive and burdensome. Food is unclean, death (without fear), life is short.

Liberation is found by recalling the ten Buddha thoughts,[18] keeping mindful of the Buddha, Dharma, Sangha, Precepts, Renunciation, Heavenly Realm; the four places to be mindful of,[19] the four correct things to do,[20] the four kinds of preternatural knowledge,[21] the five roots of sensation (eyes, ears, nose, tongue, body), the five powers for good (faith, works, thoughts, *Samadhi* concentration and wisdom), the seven offshoots of enlightenment.[22]

The Eight Fold Path,* Sunya (the Void), the formless, the three gates to liberation,[23] the Six Crossings of the Prajna-paramita (charity, keep precepts, perseverance, be energetic, Zen meditation, wisdom), the six spiritual attainments,[24] the eighteen transformations,[25] all of these items must be carefully considered.

Thus the Buddhist Canon says:

When the heart-mind is controlled,
All things become effortless.

2. Distinguishing true from false manifestations.

There are two parts to distinguishing various manifestations of roots. First, you must know how to recognize false roots; second, you must discern the truly good images.

First, what is meant by erotic and false images? If you the practitioner while doing all the Zen meditations as described above, according to the conditions in which the manifestations occur, feel limbs and torso to be agitated or trembling, or your body feels heavy, as if you were carrying a heavy load, or if you sometimes feel light and ready to fly away, or to be tied up, nodding and falling into a sound sleep, much too cold or very hot, or if you have all sorts of distracting thoughts, envisioning many strange realms and worlds, or if your mind feels darkened and stupid, or you become aware of evil thoughts arising, including distractions or confused thoughts of extraneous good deeds, thoughts which make you happy to go do them, or very sad and depressed, or thoughts occur that are so terrifying that your hair stands on end, or much too joyful so that you are confused and inebriated by them, all such thoughts are evil or bad Dharma. If they occur during Zen meditation, they are by definition lewd and false thoughts.

All of these erotic images that occur when you are doing Zen, if you are attached to them, will necessarily bring with them the ninety-five kinds of demonic spirits. How easy it is to be turned upside down and lose one's mind in thinking about them. It could also happen that evil spirits, seeing your absorption in their depraved Dharma, will increase their power and hold on you, causing all sorts of defiling images to arise in your mind, tainting your Zen meditation and your wisdom, changing the quality of your spiritual achievements so that you are able to please people of worldly attachments.

When they see you, they will say that you are a person who has "Attained the Tao," and they will choose to follow you and follow our teachings. Your inner heart-mind is perverted, if you follow such a path. What you transmit will be the way of demons. When you come to the end of your life, you will not be with the Buddha, and when reborn, you will become a *Preta* Hungry Ghost.

If when practicing (Zen) you follow evil Dharma, you will descend into (Buddhist) hell. If you want to know the causal conditions for the above, read the ninety-six forms of scriptures that are outside the Buddhist path, and there you will see the above things clearly.

You the practitioner, if while perfecting your "Stop" Samatha and "Look" Vipasyana, if you wish to prove that you are indeed practicing Zen, and all this sort of erotic and false images arise, you must treat them for what they are. How can you do this? If you know what is *Sunya* emptiness and what is false, and with a genuine heart-mind you do not receive or act on them, of necessity you must utterly destroy them. If you are not able to cut them off, then you must use "Stop" and "Look" effectively, i.e., destroy them by looking at them (for what they are), and then utterly smash them.

Second, you must understand which are the truly good phenomena which sprout during Zen meditation. If while you are sitting in Zen meditation many phenomena occur that are not like those described above, i.e., all such evil Dharma, when true *Samadhi* occurs, your response to it will reflect the phenomenon of Zen concentration. You will feel empty, bright, clear and clean. Your inner heart-mind will be filled with joy, a happiness which will gradually fill your entire being.

There will be no hindrance or obstacle, the compassionate heart-mind will open and sprout, faith and respect will increase and grow, the mind filled with discerning wisdom, body and heart-mind supple and calm, empty and detached in a wondrously subtle way. You will find the outer world oppressive, *Asamskrta* no longer acting on you and no longer an object of desire. You can enter it and come back at will, such is the manifestation of true Zen meditation.

For instance, when you are together with a wicked person, the continuing impression will be of unpleasantness, whereas when you are with a good person you will see their inner beauty. The distinguishing of evil and good roots and their manifestations will have the same results within you.

3. Using "Stop" "Look" meditation continuously to nourish good roots

If you would like to continuously nourish all sorts of good roots while sitting in meditation, at the moment when all good roots are manifest, you must use both "Stop" Samatha and "Look" Vipasyana methods to nourish them and make them improve and increase. How does one practice making them increase? When it is easier to use "Stop" Samatha to nourish good roots, then use "Stop" methods. When it is more beneficial to use "Look" Vipasyana, then use "Look" methods. One should use them according to the general description given in the above passages

---

1. Note that Buddhism, and subsequent Taoist practice, recognize three realms of awareness, i.e., the desire realm, color or form realm, and the realm that transcends form *wu se Jie*, (Sanskrit: *arupya-dhatu*). The desire realm includes of covetousness, lust, profit and fame. The stage between "desire realm" and "form realm," called *wei dao di deng ding* (not yet at the stage of Samadhi) brings about worrisome thoughts, called *fannao* in Chinese, *bonno* in Japanese (Skt.: klesa). See Sekiguchi: 1992, p. 96.

2. Samadhi, see Inagaki: 1988, p. 268.

3. The thirty-six bodily parts to be contemplated are the hair of the head, the bodily hair, nails, teeth, pupils of the eyes, tears, saliva, eyelids (closed in sleep), urine, feces, dirt, sweat, rough skin, soft skin, blood, flesh, muscles, sinews, bones, tendons, marrow, fat, oil (grease), brains, membranes, liver, gall bladder, intestines, stomach, spleen, two kidneys, heart, lungs, womb, triple warmers, red saliva and white saliva. See Sekiguchi:1992, p. 96.

4. The sixteen special victories, "juroku tokusho," effected by concentrating on breathing are being conscious of breath as short, long, flowing through the body, stopping the body from moving, awareness of joy, happiness, movement of the heart-mind, stopping the heart-mind, awareness of the mind itself, commanding the heart to be happy, command-ing the heart to be at peace, commanding the heart to let go, not to be always moving, to cut off karmic deeds, to leave behind karmic deeds, and to completely annihilate karmic (selfish, desire motivated) activities.

5. The nine visualizations, or images to be conceived under this category are the bowls, congealed green blood, mould, splattered blood, rotten pus, spit, body torn apart, bones, and searing flames.

6. Note that beginner's Zen here is a special term referring to the practitioner who is still overcoming the five desires (see note 7 below) of the "desire realm," as well as the person who is in the second stage of "form realm," before *Samadhi* awakening. In traditional Zen practice "beginner's Zen" comprises five elements: awakening, "looking" or contemplating (Vipasyana), delight, joy (in meditation), and finally reaching Samadhi. See Sekiguchi: 1982, p. 97.

7. These images become an important part of Buddhist iconography as seen in Tibetan Tankha depicting the terrifying *Yidam*, protective spirits of Tantric Buddhism. E.g., Panden Lhamo, Machin, Danjen, and Mahakala are seen snatching away the heart, intestines, brains, eyes, as reminders to purify the heart-mind before meditation. Ed. note.

8. Wealth, sex, food and drink, fame.

9. The eight things to "let go:" using inner mind to judge the exterior, using mental concepts to judge the exterior, all conceptual images, liberation from "emptiness," liberation from attempts to know the void, Liberation of non-acquisition, liberation by means of the *Madhyamika* quadrilemma "there is no image, and no non-image" (do not judge the act of existence or the act of judging existence to be real), and the total annihilation of all images, which leads to *Samadhi*, quieting mind and body during meditation.

10. The twelve *Nidanas* or causes for non-enlightenment are: *Avidya*, ign of the Four Noble Truths, *Samskara*, predisposition to karmic or selfish *Vijnyana* or initial consciousness, *Namarupa*, naming forms, *Sadayatana*, senses and intellect, *Sparsa*, contact between senses and external thing, *Vedana*, the act of sensing, *Trsna*, thirst for things sensed, *Upadana*, grasping the thing, *Bhava*, holding on to existence, *Jati*, birth, and *Jara-marana*, old age, sickness, death.

11. The five *skandas* or things scanned by mind are matter and form, perception, conceiving of mental images, judgment and will, and the mind as consciously knowing.

12. The six senses, eyes, eyes, ears, nose, tongue, body, mind, and the six things perceived by them, color, sound, smell, taste, touch, and Dharma (concepts).

13. The six senses, six objects of sense, (as in note 12) and the mind's consciousness of these actions as distinct. See Sekiguchi: 1982, p. 97.

14. The ten powers or *Shili* (Skrt., *Dasa-balani*, Jpn., *Juriki*) give perfect knowledge of right from wrong, the karmic deeds of all sentient beings, (the past, present and future), all forms of meditation, the roots of practical wisdom, wisdom to overcome obstacles and liberate all sentient beings, the different levels of existence, of Buddhist practice, the wisdom to perceive at what level of perfection a person is, wisdom to destroy all evil passions. See Inagaki: 1986, p. 156.

15. The *Catvari vaisaradyani*, (Chin., *Siwusuowei*, Jpn., *Shimushoi*), namely: 1) for a Buddha, fearlessness in asserting he/she has attained enlightenment, destroyed all defilements, showing others what hinders their enlightenment, and expounding how to attain liberation; 2) for a Bodhisattva, dauntlessly expounding scriptures and phrases learned from his/her master; giving more profound teachings to those who are well rooted, countering attacks on Buddhist teachings; and giving appropriate answers to questions asked.

16. The eighteen uncommon Dharma powers include the ten powers and four fearless qualities described in notes 14 and 15, plus overcoming the three kinds of images (self, distractions, conditional causes), and the Buddha's great compassion.

17. The term "108 forms of Samadhi liberation" is used here as a generic term for the various practices of theMahayana tradition. 108 is a cosmic number representing the 36 heavens, and 72 sacred places of earth. See Sekiguchi, p. 98.

18. The foregoing items list the ten concepts that the Buddha kept in mind, i.e., impermanence, suffering, no ego, as stated in the text. See Sekiguchi, p. 98.

19. The four things to contemplate after the mind has become tranquil from Samatha Vipasyana Zen meditation: the body as defiled, feelings as deceptive, the heart-mind as always changing, things as impermanent. See Inagaki, p. 299

20. The four things to do after contemplating the four things in note 19: i.e., stop evil deeds in the present, don't let evil deeds occur in the future, do only good deeds, and strive to increase good deeds for others.

21. The four bases for insightful or preternatural knowledge that develop from the practice of Samatha-Vipasyana meditation: i.e., spiritualize the will, actions, judgmental and intuitive mind by awakening wisdom and compassion.

22. The seven ways to cultivate true wisdom are to distinguish true from false Dharma, strive to practice true Dharma, rejoice in it, be comfortable and not strained in practice, mindful, focused, with no karmic or selfish motivated deeds.

23. The prior three terms, i.e., Samadhi, Sunya, formless are the three "non-doings," paths to *Gedatsu*, liberation.

24. The *Sad abiznya,* six spiritual powers which are attained by practicing Zen Samadhi are to change the body's form at will, see with heaven's eyes (anywhere at any distance), hear with heaven's ears (anything at any distance), know others thoughts, know former lives and deeds, and destroy completely all evil passions.

25. Eighteen manifestations or appearances that a Buddha and a Bodhisattva are able to change into. The iconography deriving from this theory are especially evident in Tantric Buddhism, the Tankha paintings of Tibet.

8. DISCERNING MARA'S DEMONIC WORK

The Sanskrit word *Mara* in Chinese language means "He who kills." Mara is the demonic power who steals from the practitioner of Zen meditation any merit or benefit, because he slays the life of wisdom. What is the meaning of "The works of the demon?" The goal of the Buddha is to lead you out of the mode of all sentient beings into Nirvana. The work of the demon Mara is to destroy the compassionate roots of all sentient beings so that they are continuously adrift in the cycle of life and death. If you calm your heart and enter the way of compassion, the higher your level of compassion, the more does the demon's opposition grow. Thus it is necessary for the compassionate person to recognize the demon's work.

There are four kinds of demons: demons of worry, demons of darkness,[1] the demon of death, and *Guei shen* demons who appear in the form of spirits. The first three are generic demonic powers which appear typically in the affairs of the world. We need not discuss them here. The phenomenon of the demonic spirit, however, is something that you must be aware of, and so we shall now describe it. There are three kinds of demonic spirits, the *Shomi* (Chn. *Jingwei*) that assume animal shapes, the *Taitei* (Chn. *Tuiti*) that cause internal distress, and Mara the demon of temptation.

The *Jingwei* demons appear in the form of the twelve animals of the zodiac, who change and take on all sorts of shapes and forms. Sometimes they appear as young men and women, sometimes as elderly apparitions from the past. Their bodily guise is quite frightening, never appearing in quite the same shape, thereby disturbing and tempting the practitioner.

Each of these *Jingwei* spirits when they disturb the meditator, must come in accord with a specific time, which is an easy way of identifying them. Those which mainly come during the *Mao* watch (3:00 to 5:00 A.M.) come as rabbit or deer demons. The *chen* watch (5:00 to 7:00 AM) are dragons, the *Si* watch (7:00 to 9:00 A.M.) are snakes, the *Wu* watch (9:00 to 11:00) are horses, donkeys and camels; the *Wei* watch (11:00 A.M. to 1:00 P.M.) are sheep; the *Shen* watch (1:00 to 3:00 P.M.) are monkeys; the *Yu* watch (3:00 to 5:00 P.M.) are chickens and crows; the *Xu* watch (5:00 to 7:00 P.M.) are dogs and wolves; the *Hai* watch (9:00 to 11:00 P.M.) are pigs; and the *Zi* watch (11:00 P.M. to 1:00 A.M.) are rats.

If you the practitioner foresee the predictable hour at which they appear, then all you need do is call the name of the animal demon, and shout in a loud voice, and it will disappear.

The *Tuiti* demons who upset us also appear in many forms, provoking us during Zen practice, crawling over our face and head, stinging and tickling our limbs, clutch and pull at our lower limbs, grasping our bodies as we practice, endlessly by talk and chatter disturbing us as we meditate, also taking on multiple forms of animals, in many different shapes and sizes. When they come to disturb you, the practitioner of Zen, you must be fully aware of what they are, and with your whole heart and mind close your eyes and scold them as follows:

I hereby recognize you, Jambu-dvipa demons,[2]
Eaters of fire and incense;
Candle stealing Kicha demons,
Eyes filled with lust,
You delight in breaking all rules.
I now have kept the precepts;
In the final end I do not fear you.

If you are a monk or nun, read the five commandments here. If you are a lay person, recite the Triple Refuge prayer (I take refuge in the Buddha, Dharma, Sangha), the five rules and the eight precepts, etc. The demons will crawl away defeated and subdued. There are many other methods like this one for getting rid of troublesome images and phenomena, such as formula for purification and exorcism found in Zen texts, in the Buddha's words.

Finally, it is Mara himself who comes to tempt and disturb you, the practitioner, taking on many changes to do so. There are three kinds of sense data for each of the five senses, used to destroy the compassionate heart-mind of the meditator: i.e., color, sound, fragrance, taste, and touch are used to scare, attract, or confuse the meditator. The first is to use the five senses and their objects to scare the meditator. The second is to elicit emotional attachments to make the meditator's heart-mind give rise to love for sense objects. The third is to use things that are neither fearful or attractive, very common and ordinary sensory data, so as to confuse the practitioner. This is why the name of the demon Mara is "The Slayer," or again "The flowery arrow," or "The five arrows,"[3] because he shoots at the heart-mind through the five senses and the feelings.

Concerning the three kinds of mental realms that can be generated from allowing one color or formal sense images, these (image realms) can confuse you while meditating, or they can draw you into a world of emotional attachment. For instance, they can make images of your mother and father, brothers and sisters, the many Buddhas, and upright men and women all appear together in your mind, a very attractive fantasy world indeed, keeping the heart-mind quite busy in this realm of formal image. Concerning the visualized realms that generate feelings of fear in you when meditating, these produce such sights as snarling tigers, wolves and lions, *Raksasa* (blood eating) demons, and all kinds of fearful images coming to upset your meditation practice. Images that neither frighten or attract you during practice, but appear as rather ordinary can also upset your mind while meditating, making you lose your Zen concentration. Therefore all of these images are called Mara demons.

They also can change into all sorts of pleasant or repulsive sounds, fragrant or fetid odors, delicious or disgusting tastes, sad or joyful fantasy worlds, coming to intrude into your human body. Such are the deeds of the demon Mara. The variety of images are so many that we cannot describe them in concrete detail.

To sum this all up briefly, whether there arise images of the world through the five senses, disturbances during your meditation, making you lose your way of compassion, bringing up all sorts of troubles and worries, these are all troops of the demon Mara. They are able to destroy you, making the Buddha's way seem dull and ordinary, kindling feelings of greed, lust, depression and sorrow, hatred, anger, sleep, and so forth, all indeed obstacles to the Dharma path. A hymn in the Buddhist Canon describes it thus:

Desire is the first of (Mara's) troops,
Then depression, sadness are second,
Hunger and thirst are third,
Yearning for love is fourth,
Sleepiness and langur are fifth,
Anxiety and fear are sixth,
Doubts and regrets are seventh,
Anger and resentment eighth,
Gainful profit (as mind filling) ninth,
Pride and despising others tenth,
If there are so many troops in this army,

To oppress, annihilate the Sangha of monks,
Then I shall use my Zen and wisdom powers,
To destroy all your troops and armies,
Achieve fulfillment of the Buddha path,
Lead over and liberating all human beings.

When you, the meditator, are able to be aware of the demon Mara's works, then you must on your own overcome them.

There are two ways to do this: The practice of "Stop" Samatha can stop them. All that you see, all the images from the outside, good or bad, are from the realm of the demon Mara. You must realize that they are void and empty. Do not become attached to them or fear them. Also, do not focus on them, discriminating and judging them. Let the mind rest in solitude. They will disappear of themselves.

The practice of "Look" Vipasyana can do away with them. If you see any of the things described above, all of the various Mara realms, and if they aren't dispelled by Samatha "Stop" meditation, then you must turn back and use Vipasyana "Look." I.e., focus on your heart-mind, seeing that it is not something that exists as an object in itself (i.e., mind has no "place" of itself), and that therefore there is nothing in it to cause worry. If you look at it thus, (i.e., the worries only have existence in the mind, not in reality, and the mind itself exists only when in the act of worrying), then while practicing "Look" Vipasyana the images will disappear and be obliterated.

But if no matter what the images do not go away, then you must continue to meditate steadfastly, not letting fear or annoyance arise. Even at the risk of sacrificing your life, keep your upright heart unmoved. Realize that neither the demon world or the Buddha world are the ultimate reality. It is as if the demon world is a part of the Buddha world, one and not distinct, and thus as for the demon world there is nothing to be cast aside, and as for the Buddha world, there is nothing to be gained. The Buddha world will thereupon come to the forefront of your consciousness, and the demon world will evaporate.

Put in another way, if you see that demonic fantasies aren't wiped out, don't let yourself be depressed. If you see that they are obliterated, don't be overjoyed. The reason is because it has never once been seen that a demon transformed into a tiger or wolf ate a person sitting in Zen meditation. Nor has it ever happened that a demon who took on the appearance of a man or woman could be taken as husband or wife. You must realize that all mental images are pure fantasy.

The foolish do not understand this. Fear and distress arise in their heart-mind, and then avarice, causing the mind to be disturbed and Zen concentration lost, giving rise to anxiety and even psychosis. Such conditions are not due to the Mara demon, they are caused by the practitioner herself or himself. I.e., lack of wisdom and internal psychosis are in the meditator, not the demon.

To sum up, if all of these demonic illusions continue to bother you, and cannot be got rid of over a period of several months or years, then you must be of firm heart and mind, be firm and strong in maintaining correct concepts, not grieving giving your life to do so, not harboring sadness or anger. You should chant the Mähayana sutras, recite the *Dharani* mantras,[4] and while reciting them keep in mind the Three Treasures (Buddha, Dharma, Sangha). When coming out of Zen meditation, you should likewise chant the *Dharani* to protect yourself, the litanies of repentance and remorse, (Jpn. *Sangezangi*), and recite the *Pratimoksa* rules of the monk or nun. Evil is no match for the good, and in the long run will be destroyed.

The varieties of demonic deeds are so many that there is no end to talking about them, yet we must understand them well. For this reason the heart-mind of the beginner in Zen practice must be very familiar with a good and knowledgeable master, who can explain why such difficulties occur. When the demon enters the human heart-mind, the spirit becomes upset, confused, depressed or elated, which could be the cause of harm or even death of the practitioner. Sometimes they induce evil Zen meditation, satanic wisdom, communicating with bad spirits, sinister *Dharani* spells, the teaching of corrupt Dharma which the worldly rush to believe and follow, whereupon great harm is done to many people, driving compassion out of the world and destroying the True Dharma.

Since there are so many forms of demonic illusions not of a uniform nature, they cannot all be treated of as one. Here I have mentioned the most important ones, as examples to help you the practitioner of Zen meditation not to be deceived into admitting the many demonic realms of fantasy (into your consciousness).

In summary, if you wish to put aside all evil and return to the true way, you must contemplate the phenomenal aspects (the real appearance, as contrasted to the noumenal outer world not a part of willed and judged consciousness) of all Dharmas (thought images). If you learn how to practice "Stop" Samatha and "Look" Vipasyana well, then there will be bo evil image that you cannot get rid of. Thus the Buddhist Treatise says: "Except for the phenomenon of the Buddha's teaching, all of reality is the work of Mara." Thus the *Gatha* hymn relates:

Discriminating judgment, thought and image,
Are all nets of the demon Mara.
Unmoved, non-judgment,
Are the Seals of the Dharma*

*(Trans. note; the Three Dharma Seals:)
All things are transient,
All Dharma has no self,
Nirvana is tranquil solitude.

---

1. The demon of darkness, literally "the demon who leads the practitioner into the illusive world of the five Skandhas, 'form and matter, perception, concept, judgment and will, self consciousness.'"

2. The Japanese-Chinese term *Enbutai* (Yanfuti) is a transliteration of the Sanskrit word, referring to the country to the south side of the Cosmic Mt. Sumeru, to which the exorcistic phrase used here exiles the demons.

3. The term "Five colorful arrows" is a metaphor for the five senses, which Mara uses as five arrows to pierce into the heart-mind of the meditator, thus destroying the effects of Zen meditation, compassion and wisdom.

4. Zen and other monks chant daily the *Da Beizhou* mantra, the Heart Sutra, the 25th Chapter of the Lotus Sutra and other texts, achieving thereby peace and stillness of mind as preparation for Zen *Samadhi* meditation. (Trans. note).

9. HEALING ILLNESS AND WORRY

You the practitioner, while trying to calm your heart-mind or perfecting the Way (of wisdom and compassion), may become ill either from external causes such as the four elements (chilling wind, burning fire, drenching water, ills from the earth) or from a misuse of breathing and other meditation methods. This latter form of illness occurs either because you have not been able to regulate your practice properly, including the use of body, breath and heart-mind in meditation, or for other internal and external causes that contravene to make you ill. If you perform your sitting Zen practice properly, and if you can use your heart-mind with compassion, the 404 kinds of illness[1] will be healed and eliminated by nature (quite naturally).

But if you lose control of your heart-mind, then you arouse the 404 kinds of ailments. For this reason when practicing by yourself or teaching others, you should know well the origin of illness, and understand the method of healing sickness by visualization within the heart-mind during Zen sitting. If you don't know how to heal infirmity, then one day when you get sick you will not only be impeded from practicing the way (of Zen compassion) but you may also imperil your life.

To heal illness you must learn two things, i.e., how to diagnose the disease from its manifestations, and the method to heal it. First let us discuss diagnosing illness from manifest phenomena. Though there are many illnesses caused by blockages within the body, there are only two generic sources for disorders: over supply or deficiency of the four elements, or illness in the five internal organs (liver, heart, lungs, kidneys, spleen).[2]

When an illness occurs due to one of the four elements (i.e., from natural causes), such as an excess of the earth element (foods, microbes, organisms that live in the earth), then swelling and cramps are deep and hard to bear. The body becomes withered and thin, and from this condition 101 other ills are born. When the water element is in excess, then fluids and bile fill the bowels, fod annd drink are not digested, stomach disorders and dysentery occur, and another 101 ills are generated. When the fire element is in excess, then there is sweating and shivering and high fever, the all the limbs of the body hurt, the mouth is dry and the nose congested, loose bowels and frequent urine, and the whole body feels obstructed, from whence another 101 ills arise. If there is an excess of wind, the body feels as if it were suspended in space, battered about, hurting, itching and pressed, stomach upset and nauseated, trying but unable to cough, and from this condition another 101 ills occur. Thus the Buddhist Sutra says:

> If one of the four elements is out of order,
> 101 afflictions will be born.

Thus, if the four elements are irregular, 404 ailments will arise in an instant. When the four great elements give rise to sickness, each has its own different qualities. Therefore it is necessary that while you are sitting in meditation, you must see yourself examining them (the qualities) in your mind's visualization.

Second, we must understand the symptoms of illness deriving from the five internal organs. Those ailments coming from the heart (the element fire) are mostly manifested in the warmth and cold of the body (perspiring and shivering), as well as pain and dryness of the mouth, etc. This is because the heart is master of the mouth. Illnesses that are born from the lungs are manifest in the stomach filled with gas, the four limbs ache, the heart stifled and the nose plugged up, etc. This is because the lungs are master of the nose.

Illnesses born of the liver are due mostly to excessive joy, sadness or unhappiness, sorrowful thoughts and vengeful anger. The head hurts and the eyes are clouded, because the liver rules over the eyes. Ailments born of the spleen appear in the body, top of the head and face, vertigo or dizziness as if blown in the wind, food and drink lose all taste, because the spleen is master of the tongue.

Diseases born of the kidneys are manifest in a soar throat and bronchitis, the stomach is heavy and the ears buzz, because the kidneys are the ruler of the ears. The illnesses produced from the five internal organs are many; each has its own symptoms and manifestations. You must visualize each one and examine it while sitting in Zen meditation, and then you can naturally diagnose it.

As seen above, there are many kinds of illness that rise from the four elements and afflict the five storage organs. The causes are not the same, and the symptoms too many to be mentioned here in detail. You who practice meditation, if you wish to perfect the "Stop" Samatha and "Look" Vipasyana Dharma path, to rid yourself of the ailments that make illness occur, must know well the reasons why they arise.

These two kinds of ailments (i.e., from nature's four elements and the body's five organs) afflict you interiorly and exteriorly for related causes. If you are afflicted externally by cold, dampness, wind or heat, if you are not careful about what you drink and eat, and you feel ill in both places (inside and outside), you can be sure that the cause is an external one. But if it is due to not perfecting the way you use your heart-mind, and in "looking" at your movement (of breath) you were wrong or coarse, or because you didn't know when it was time to develop the method of Samadhi you weren't sure of the proper way to use it, (meditating without a master or teacher) and if you get sick under these conditions, then you can be sure that the sickness is from an internal cause.

Next, there are three kinds of illness which you can contract, each with different sets of causes. The first kind is caused by excess or deficiency in the Four Elements of Nature and the Five Internal Organs, which were treated in concrete detail above. The second are disorders caused by demonic spirits. The third are diseases which are due to things we have done in the past.[3] With all of these many illnesses, if they are treated when they first occur, then it is much easier to heal them. But if they are left untreated for a lenghty period of time, then the illness becomes chronic, the body feeble, and the healing process is much more difficult.

The second thing for you to learn is how is to treat an illness, after diagnosing its origin and causes, i.e., what methods must be used to heal it. There are many methods for healing illness. To describe the most efficient way, we need not go beyond "Stop" Samatha and "Look" Vipasyana, these two methods.

How can you use "Stop" Samatha to heal illness? A (Zen) Master once said:

> You need only bring the heart-mind to focus on the location of the ailment, and you will be able to heal it. The reason why this is so is because the mind is master over what happens throughout our life, both rewards and punishments. It is like the ruler of a kingdom who, when he arrives in a certain place, all the thieves flee in terror.

A Zen master also said:

> There is a spot just below the belly button called the *Udana*, or by others the *Xia Dantian* Lower Cinnabar Field,'[4] an inch below the navel. If you can concentrate your heart-

mind and keep it focused on this spot for a length of time (ed. note: Buddhist Samatha and Taoist centering meditation both use this place as as a point of focus), most illnesses will be healed.

Again a Zen master said:

> Always keep your mind focused on the bottom of your feet, don't worry about where you will walk, stand, recline or sleep. This practice will heal all sorts of ailments, the reason being that people get sick when the Four Elements are not regulated. This lack of regularity is caused by the mind being pre-occupied with thoughts and worries in the upper part of the body. If the heart-mind is kept peacefully focused in the lower part of the body, the Four Elements will be regulated quite naturally, and a plethora of ills prevented.

On another occasion a Zen master said:

> If only you realized that knowledge of all Dharma (words, concepts and images) is empty and non-existent! Thus by letting go of the image of yourself as ill, the ailment will be abandoned and thus arrested and stopped. Many ailments are healed in this way, for which reason it is often due to the heart-mind excessive thinking and imagining that the four elements are drummed to excess and illnesses occur. If the heart mind is made peaceful, the ailments leave

Thus the *Vimalakirti-nirdesa* Sutra says:[5]

> What is the origin of sickness?
> Too many attachment to the outside.
> How stop this attachment to causes?
> Tell the heart there's nothing to gain.

You can see from all of these examples that there are many explanations of how to use "Stop," Samatha focusing, to heal illness.

Thus you the practitioner must understand that out of compassion you should perfect the methods of using "Stop" Samatha to heal all sorts of ailments.

How can you use "Look" Vipasyana to heal illness? You who would understand the use of Vipasyana visualization to heal sickness must listen to the words of the (Zen) master who said:

Look at the heart mind and visualize
The six kinds of breath which heal disease.
This is how Vipasyana visualization mends ills.

What are the six kinds of breath? They are the (meditative) sounds *Chui*, *Hu*, *Xi*, *Ha*, *Xü*, and *Si*.[6] Each of the sounds are to be vocalized between the mouth and the lips, while visualizing with the heart mind (the colors, and organs), as a kind of *upaya* skillful means for healing by circulating them (colors, breath, and sound) with the minds eye through the various organs. If performed while sitting in Zen meditation, if you feel cold, respond with the *Chui* sound; if you feel heat or stress, respond with the *Hu* sound. If you want to heal illness, *Chui* eliminates cold, and *Hu* dispels heat. *Xi* alleviates pain, and is used to heal wind ailments. *Ha* chases away worry and is used to make *Qi* breath (mind's focus) circulate downward. *Xu* expels phlegm and also eliminates stuffed bowels or constipation (a sign of arrogance). *Xi* revitalizes fatigue. If you use them to heal the five storage organs, *Hu* and *Chui* these two breath-sounds can be used to heal the heart; *Xu* heals the liver; *Ha* heals the lungs; *Xi* heals the spleen, and *Si* the kidneys.[7]

Another Zen master taught that if you are able to use "Look" Vipasyana meditation with compassion, you will develop the ability to use twelve kinds of breath to heal all sorts of ailments, as follows: visualize breath circulating through the upper body, through the lower body, fill the body with breath, circulate fiery breath through the body, increase the length of each breath, expel and eliminate breath from the body, circulate warm breath, cold breath, subtle breath, hold the breath, peaceful and quiet breath, healing or mending breath. These twelve kinds of breath are all born from "Look" Vipasyana meditation by visualization in the heart-mind.

Now let us look at each of these twelve breaths and see by way of example what phenomena they can heal:

Circulating breath through the upper body heals heaviness,
Through the lower body heals light-headedness or dizziness.
Filling the body with Qi breath heals the shriveled and sterile, fiery breath heals stuffed bowels (and arrogance).
Lengthening the breath heals consumption and injury,
(i.e., see breath move slowly through the affected area)
Stopping or Holding breath keeps diseases from spreading.
Warm breath heals cold, cool breath heals fever. Propelled breath opens blocked passages and knots. Holding the breath heals trembling and shivering. Harmonizing the breath heals disorders of the Four Elements. Healing breath is the source for mending the Four Elements.

If you use these breathing methods with compassion, you will easily be able to heal many ailments. But if you lose the proper way to employ them, all sorts of illnesses will arise, as you will find out from practice.

Yet another Zen master has said:

Visualizing with the mind's eye in Vipasyana meditation,
Makes you able to heal all illness.
Thus when a person is afflicted with chills (shivering)
Visualize that from within your body flames of Qi arise,
Which you can use to heal the affliction.

This is similar to the passage found in the *Samyuktagama* Sutra,[8] "On seventy-two esoteric ways to heal spiritual illnesses," which methods are amply described therein.

Another Zen master says:

> You need only use 'Stop' and 'Look' to examine and judge the state of the Four Elements within the body. Visualize that neither the illness itself or the concept of sickness in the mind exist by themselves. If the myriad ills are not healed, it is due to the fact that you erred in diagnosing it.

There are many different ways of diagnosing illness, and using Vipasyana visualization to heal them.

> Perform the diagnosis well,
> There is no ailment that cannot be healed.
> Each must have its own different cause.

Thus you must realize that the two methods of "Stop" and "Look" meditation, if earned well and used with compassion, can heal every kind of ailment.

However, recently people have become less well rooted in meditation, and the use of Samatha "Stop" and Vipasyana "Look" methods have for the most part not been perfected. Nor are they practiced by the worldly. Further, since they don't attain to such meditative skills, heterodox forms of *Qi* breathing techniques and abstention from cereal starches are unfortunately springing up.[9]

Medicines derived from minerals and herbs are used to good effect in healing illness, and can be taken with food and drink. If the illness is due to demonic, i.e., spiritual causes, you must strengthen the heart-mind and add the use of intoned prayers (Mantra) to assist in healing the ailment.[10] If the illness is caused by karmic deeds of the past (willed or deliberate acts to harm others), then you must increase works of assisting others, cultivate happiness, chant litanies of repentance,[11] whereupon the affliction will disappear by itself.

If you the practitioner learn to do these two ways (Samatha Vipasyana) of healing illness with a single mind, then you can put them to practice yourself and also teach others to do so; how much the more effective they will become by repeated concrete practice. But if we haven't learned any of them, then when illness occurs it won't be healed, and not only will you have to put aside practicing the correct method, but you must also consider that you may be endangering your own life. How dare think of teaching others!

Therefore those who wish to practice the method of "Stop" Samatha and "Look" Vipasyana meditation must understand well (with compassion) the way of healing illness by visualization within the heart-mind. The ways of healing illness with the inner mind are very many, too many to be written down in detail here. If you want to know more about this, then you should conduct a further survey (of Zen masters). The explanations given above contain only a general idea; if you really want to use (healing methods), I fear there is not yet a complete manual.

You ask: If one uses the heart mind to heal illness while sitting in Zen, will there be definite results or not?

Response: If you concretely put these ten methods into practice, there cannot but be good results.

The ten methods (for healing) are: faith, practice, diligence, hard work, constancy, diagnose the cause of illness, *Upaya* skillful means, continual practice, know when to use and when to discard (a method), compassionate care, recognize obstacles.

What does it mean to have faith? It means to believe that this method of healing illness will surely work. What does practice mean? It means to use it frequently. Diligently means to work energetically without passing over all difficulties until the illness is healed. What does it mean to constantly concentrate on the cause alone? It means to focus the heart-mind and continually visualize without letting the mind be distracted by other things.

What does it mean to diagnose the cause of the illness? It means to diagnose the cause correctly as was explained above in detail. What is meant by *Upaya* skillful means? It means circulating the breath with the mind's eye through the area where the cause of the illness exists, until by compassion superior results are obtained, without loss of your own well-being.

What is meant by continual practice? It means that while using the healing method no significant results are yet seen, you don't count the days and months but continue the practice without tiring. What does "knowing when to use and discard" mean? It means to know that when there is benefit the method should be used diligently, but when there is harm, it should be discarded.

One must use the heart-mind with subtlety to achieve healing. What is meant by knowing when to protect? It means to use compassion to recognize causes that are not beneficial and separate the sick person from them. What does it mean to recognize obstacles? It means that when gain or healing occurs, you shouldn't easily disclose it to others, since it has not yet been proven, or less others get jealous and criticize you for it. If you use these ten methods, the diseases will certainly be healed by your methods, they will not be empty or in vain.

---

1. The 404 kinds of ailments are derived from the Indian Buddhist tradition, i.e., there are 101ailments for each of the four elements, as explained below.

2. The five internal storage organs are thought to be a primary source of bodily ailments in traditional Chinese medicine. Zhi Yi explains how each organ effects health below.

3. Note that the word used in the Chinese text, *ye* for deeds or things done in the past is also the word used to translate the Sanskrit word *karma.* The ordinary English use of the word "Karma" for fate (as in "it is my Karma") misunderstands the Sanskrit sense of "Karma." Human deeds that are known and willed fall under the title "karma," i.e., they bear retribution some time in the future. Thus deed or karma is the cause of recycling, or retribution, not some unknownfate. Deeds that arise from the vegetable or animal activities of the human body, such as necessary sleep when tired, necessary nutrition, all involuntary functions, are not the cause of "Karma." (Trans. note).

4. The Xia Dantian is a Taoist term for the centering place in the body, approximately two inches below the navel, and three inches within, which is the place of focus in both Taoist and Buddhist meditation. For a Taoist description of this place and the meditations performed in the Taoist contemplative tradition, see Saso, M., *The Gold Pavilion*, Boston: Tuttle Press, 1995.

5. The *Vimalakirti-nirdesa Sutra,* (Chn., *Jingming Jing,* Jpn., *Yuima* and also *Jomyo Kyo*) is attributed to a rich lay man of Vaisala, India, who was famous for his deep understanding of Mahayana doctrines. It is in the Taisho Buddhist Canon, T. 14.

6. These mentally conceived sounds come from the Taoist meditative tradition, showing the mutual influence of the two great contemplative religions on Mt. Tiantai in Jejiang province, where Zhi Yi is thought to have composed this treatise. Each sound refers to a color, a direction, an internal organ, visualized as part of the healing process, See below.

7. The sounds and their correspondence to the five storage organs as taught by Zhi Yi differ slightly from the Taoist meditative tradition, for which see *Gold Pavilion* (Saso, 1995, Ch. 3). Healing in the Taoist system attaches a color, one of five Chinese elements, direction, season and symbol to each of the mantric sounds:

Liver	wood	east	green	spring	dragon	Xu	
Heart	fire	south	red	summer	phoenix	Hu,	
Lungs	metal	west	white	autumn	tiger	Ha	
Spleen	earth	center	yellow	human in the center		Xi	
Kidneys	water	north	purple	winter	turtle	Si	(Cui)

8.The "Za" or Miscellaneous Agamas are among the earliest writings in the Buddhist Scripture, found in the first two volumes of the Taisho Canon.

9. The Chinese text, used by Sekiguchi (p. 118) leaves out this passage. It is found, however, in the Taisho version of the Buddhist Canon, Vol. 46, # 1915, p. 472a.

10. The use of *zhou* or mantra in the Buddhist and Taoist traditions of China and East Asia is seen as an aid to the healing of illness by visualization. The sick person and the monk in attendance invoke the presence of good, compassionate spiritual forces to expel the illness, helping strengthen the patient to recover.

11. The term *Chanhui* means repentance, but in fact these texts consist in long lists of the names of saints, Bodhisattvas and blessed ones, the recitation of which creates a kind of mandala of blessing around the praying person. Both Taoist and Buddhist practice makes extensive use of *Chanhui* as a prelude to prayer.

10. THE FRUIT OF TRUE MEDITATION

1. The Correct Way to Meditate

If you the practitioner while perfecting your "Stop" "Look" meditation have reached the point where you are able to understand that all Dharma is born from the heart-mind, and that external causes and conditions are void and false, unreal and therefore empty, and if you know they are empty you realize that there is no Dharma that is attainable (existent), it is but a name and external appearance, this is "Nature really exists Samatha (i.e., stop the idea)." At this point you will see that above you there are no fruits to be sought from the Buddha, and below you there are no sentient beings to be saved. This state is called "Entering contemplation of *Sunya* the void through the unreal false things of the world" (Jpn. *Jyuge nitsu ku*, Chn. *Cong jia ru kong*). It is also called "Twofold Truth," (Jpn. *Nitai*, Chn. *Erdi*, absolute and conventional truth), "The Wisdom Eye,"[1] and "Wisdom in all things, (Jpn. *Issaichi*, Chn. *Yichie Zhihui*).[2] But if you remain in this kind of contemplative practice, you will fall into the mode of a Shramana or Pratyeka practitioner.[3] Thus the Lotus Sutra says:

> The Shramanas and other practitioners say,
> 'If we hear of the Pure Land Buddha teachings,
> To instruct and save all sentient beings,
> We are unhappy, because each and all Dharmas
> Are empty and unreal, neither born or obliterated
> Neither big or small,
> *Anasrava* undefiled, *Asamskrta* uncreated.
> Perceiving this to be so,
> We do not let joy or happiness arise.'

For this reason you must realize that if a person meditates in the state of *Asamskrta* only, the perfection of Sambodhi wisdom will never arise in his or her heart-mind.[4] Even though their powers of concentration are developed to a very high level, they will never see the Buddha nature.

If you like a Boddhisattva would assist all sentient beings cross over to the shore of wisdom, you can only do this by perfecting all Buddhist Dharma, not just *Asamskrta* concentration (no thoughts arising). You must thereupon perfect the manner of Vipasyana contemplation which comes out of the state of *Sunya* void and looks at the world of illusions. Further you must from contemplating the (Twofold, absolute and worldly) Truth realize that even though the mind is by nature empty, when it is presented with external causal conditions, all sorts of Dharma are born and arise, illusory and changing. Even though in fact you aren't caught up or focused on any one of them, still you see, hear, sense and think about them, since they appear as phenomena in which you discern differences.

Now you the practitioner, if when contemplating them, even though you know that all Dharma are in the end empty and false, if you can in this state of emptiness perfect all sorts of practices, such as planting a tree in the void (i.e., external reality), you are also able to distinguish that there are many kinds of sentient beings, all rooted in different natures and desires. Because their natures and desires are innumerable, so too the teaching of the Dharma to them is without measure.

In order to have results, you must have immeasurable eloquence, and only then will you be able to benefit the beings in the six paths of existence (humans, animals, spirits; demons, preta, asura), all sentient beings. "This is called the Samatha (stop the mind from imaging or judging) that is skilled in going after external causes."[5] One comes forth from this empty "Stopping" of vision to Vipasyana contemplating the false outside world. It is also called looking "equally" at all things without discrimination, "Dharma" eyes, and the *Doshuchi* (Chn., *Daozhongzhi*), Wisdom for the Bodhisattva Path.[6] If you remain in this state, your power of wisdom will increase, but even if you were to see the Buddha nature, you wouldn't recognize it.

Even for the Boddhisattva accomplished in following these two methods of Vipasyana "Looking," especially the second *Upaya* of contemplating the false world, are not correct ways of practicing Vipasyana contemplation. Therefore the Sutra says:

> The first two kinds of Vipasyana are *Upaya* skills,
> Thus both are empty contemplation, (only means to)
> Lead you to the first notion of Middle Way meditation,
> I.e., when looking at both sides from the center,
> (the false external and the void, empty world)
> The heart mind is isolated and extinguished,
> From whence it naturally flows into
> The Sarva-Jñana ocean of wisdom.

The Bodhisattva who wishes in a single flash of thought to master totally all Buddhist Dharma, "must perfect that kind of stopping (Samatha) which desists from judging or discriminating either of the two sides (external and internal, to be false or empty), doing this as one's practice," i.e., the middle way of correct Vipasyana meditation.[7]

How define the "correct" way of contemplation? If you are able to "Realize that the substance and nature of the heart mind is neither true nor false, and make the heart-mind desist from judging the world of external causes to be true or false, this is called 'correct' Vipasyana contemplation."

When scrutinizing the nature of the heart-mind,
Judge it to be neither void or false,
Nor judge the "Void and false" method as bad,
If you can be enlightened by this way of Zen,
Then the nature of heart-mind will acquire
Union with the middle way, totally enlightened
To the twofold truth, absolute and relative,
(*Shintai*, *Paramartha-satya*, absolute truth and
Zokutai, *Samvrti-satya*, conditioned reality).
If you can contemplate with the centered mind,
Then look out at the two realities from the center,
And also look at all Dharmas,
The Middle Way and the two realities,
Do not hold onto the Middle Way or the two realities,
Because not even the Absolute nature,
Can thereby be grasped or held onto.

This is what is called correct Zen contemplation from the Middle Way. Concerning it a hymn in the *Madhyamika Sastra* says:

All Dharmas born from external causes
I tell you, are empty.
Their names are false names,
But they also indicate the Middle Way.

If you penetrate to the deeper meaning of this hymn, not only does it explain concretely how to discern what is the correct way to do Vipasyana Zen contemplation, it also explains clearly the former two *upaya* skills (contemplating the mind as empty and the outer world as false) as related to Middle Way contemplation.

Correct Contemplation in the Middle Way gives you the "Buddha Eyes," and all forms of wisdom (Sarvajñana).

2. "Stop" Samatha, "Look" Vipasyana and Mahayana Buddhism[8]

If you persevere in this form of Vipasyana, Zen meditation and sound wisdom, you will ultimately envision the Buddha nature, abide serenely in the Mahayana way, walk steadily in the correct path, swift as the wind. If your progress is swift like the wind, you will quite naturally flow into the ocean of wisdom (Sarvajña). Once you have entered the Ocean of Wisdom, then you will be walk the Tathagatha Buddha's path, dwell in the Tathagatha's abode, wear the Buddha's clothes, sit on his throne, adorned with his dignity.[9] From the Buddha's dignity you yourself will have strength and authority, to keep the six senses pure, and enter the Buddha realm, impervious from contamination by any image or Dharma.

When protected from the stain of any Dharma image, all of the Buddhas will appear before you, and you will attain to constant awareness of Buddha's Samadhi, (a constant state of focused awareness on Absolute presence), the awareness called *Suramgama Samadhi.*[10] From this state you can attain the Samadhi of Samantabhadra (the Bodhisattva whose meditation leads to good works; he saves all sentient beings by works of compassion and wisdom; he is seen riding an elephant in Buddhist iconography), enter all the Buddha lands of the ten directions, to save all sentient beings, clean and adorn all Buddhist shrines, make offerings (i.e., putting fruit, candles, incense, Yak [dri] butter or oil lamps, Hada scarves, money, etc. on the altar of a Buddhist shrine; ed. note) in honor of all the Buddhas of the ten directions.

If you make offerings to the Buddhas of the ten directions, you must also keep the rules and teachings of the Buddhist scriptures, keeping them in concrete detail, all the practices, and Paramitas (wisdom parameters), then you will attain to sudden enlightenment of the great Bodhisattva, such as Samantabhadra, Manjusri (symbol of wisdom, pictured riding a lion, when paired with Samantabhadra), keeping company with them as friend and companion, in the eternal presence of and participating in the Dharma nature body.[11]

If you can keep yourself always aware of the physical presence of the Dharma nature in your body, then the Buddhas of the ten directions will weigh and record your achievements in the Pure Land Tusita Heavens.[12] If the Buddhas of the Ten Directions keep record of you in the Tusita Heavens, then you will be able to portray and relive (see the myth enfold of) the coming down of the spirit into the sacred mother of the Buddha, his enlightenment under the Bodhi tree, after exorcising the wrathful demon Mara, manifesting true enlightenment, correct cycling of the wheel of Dharma (life) so as to reach Nirvana, the perfection of all the Buddha's works in the ten nations (of India), which when completed allowed him to attain to the two bodies, the real and the response body (Nirmanakaya, see endnote 11), the first manifestation (in yourself) of the heart-mind abiding in the way of the Bodhisattva.

Thus the Avatamsaka Sutra (Jpn. *Kegon Kyo*, Chn. *Huayen Jing*) says (in several passages):

> The first awakening of the Boddhisattva's heart-mind
> Realizes more deeply true enlightenment,
> Masters completely all of the Dharmas,
> Knows the true nature of all things,
> The wisdom body now attained,
> Is not something realized by another
> (is realized from within myself)

Another passage reads:

> The first awakening of the Boddhisattva's heart-mind
> Attains the Tathagata body,
> From whence comes (three) limitless bodies,[13]

It also says:

> The just awakened heart-mind of a Bodhisatta
> Realizes (in himself) the eight major events
> (in the Buddhas life, i.e., coming down from Tusita Heaven,
> Conceived, and born from his mother's womb,
> Renounces the world, defeats Mara, is enlightened,
> preaches the law, passes into Nirvana).

Again it says:

> The just awakened heart-mind of a Boddhisattva
> Is the Buddha.

The Nirvana Sutra also relates:

> The first awakened mind and the master's mind
> Are the same;
> The only way they're different is,
> The first one's harder to attain.

From the Prajna-paramita Sutra:

> Oh Subhuti! (a disciple of Buddha)
> Bodhisattvas and Mahasattvas (enlightened ones)
> From the first awakening of their heart-mind
> Sit in a Mandala, (centered meditation space)
> And revolve the wheel of life.
> You must realize, the Bodhisattvas
> Are like the Buddha when they do this.

From the Lotus Sutra:

> The Dragon Lady gave Buddha a Pearl necklace
> As proof of her enlightenment.[14]

All of these illustrations from the Buddhist Scriptures show how the beginner's mind can find enlightenment and mastery of all Buddhist Dharma. This can be done, as the Prajna-paramita Sutra says, by intoning the "Ah" letter (which initiates the "A,B,C..." characters of the Sanskrit alphabet, and also serves as the gateway to all Buddhist Dharma), or the Lotus Sutra doctrine that it is enough to see an image of the Buddha to open the heart-mind of all sentient beings to enlightenment. As in the Nirvana Sutra:

Just by seeing the Buddha's nature,
One can abide in great awakening.

These examples demonstrate by the fruits shown that the beginning of a Bodhisattva's heart-mind is found in perfecting Samatha "Stop" and Vipasyana "Look" meditation.

To understand the phenomenon of the heart-mind in its final state, from the evidence of its fruits, but the sphere of perception of the ultimate mind in the end cannot be known (the ultimate mind is without concept), except, relying on the teachings of the masters, by the use of Samatha "Stop" and Vipasyana "Look" methods. The reason for this is, as the Lotus Sutra says, "Respectfully glorify the wisdom of the Buddhas; wisdom is the meaning of Vipasyana "looking," and to do this (looking) is to use Vipasyana to prove the fruit of meditation." The Nirvana Sutra also says, "To liberate the mind from always arguing the 100 phrases, this is Syakyamuni's great Nirvana, this is to use Samatha to prove the fruit of meditation."

Therefore it is said, "The *Prajna-paramita* nirvana is to constantly isolate the mind in Samadhi concentration. Focusing in Samadhi is Samatha "stopping" mental action. The Lotus Sutra says:

Although you use Vipasyana to understand the fruit of wisdom, it equally helps to use Samatha. Therefore is it said that when you reach the ultimate nirvana, the mind abiding in solitude conceptual images are obliterated, and in the end one returns to *Sunya* the void. Nirvana, though it proves the fruit of Samatha cessation, it is also useful to use Vipasyana. Therefore there are three virtues, (Dharmakaya, Prajna wisdom, and liberation), which are called the "Great Nirvana."

These two great sutras reduplicate many phrases. Their origins are different, yet their purpose the same. Samatha and Vipasyana, these two portals, if one debates their use, in the long run they are cessation of imaging, and looking with wisdom, two paths, used to prove the supreme fruit of meditation.

You the practitioner must know that the beginning, middle, and ultimate fruits of this meditation are so many that they cannot be conceived. Thus the *Konkomyo-kyo (Suvarna-prabhasa-uttama-sutra*, the "Golden Splendor" Sutra, Taisho Vol. 16, No. 663) says:

> The Tathagata of the past could not be imagined,
> The Tathagata of the now is resplendent in so many ways,
> The Tathagata of the future is eternal, indestructible.

All of these stages were the fruit of the two kinds of "Stop" and "Look" contemplation. It is for this reason that the *Hanju Zanmai* Hymn (Taisho Vol. 47, No. 1981) says:

> All the Buddhas attained liberation from the Heart-mind,
> The heart-mind that is pure and clean is called unblemished.
> Keep the five paths pure and clean, free from *Rupa* sensual images, Those who free themselves from this attain the Great Tao.

---

1. One of the five eyes or ways to apprehend the reality of Buddhist practice: the eye of the fleshly body, the heavenly eye, wisdom eye, Dharma eye and Buddha eye. The wisdom eye is defined in the preceding passage, i.e., seeing all external things and Dharma as false and empty.

2. The wisdom of a Buddha, a Shravaka or hearer of the Buddha's doctrine, and a Pratyeka Buddha or one who attains enlightenment without a teacher. The term *Sanchi* or "Three Wisdoms" is also used, meaning the wisdom of the Theravada tradition which includes the Shravaka and Pratyeka practitioner, the Bodhisattva (Mahayana tradition), and the Buddha, i.e., knowing all kinds of existence in general or discriminative aspect. See Inagaki:1986, p. 262.

3. See note 2, above. The Shramana and Pratyeka Buddha practitioners of the Theravada or Hinayana tradition are here put on a lesser level of perfection than the Mahayana monks who practice "Stop" "Look" meditation. In fact, Theravada monks too practice *Samatha Vipasyana* (Pali: *Samatta Vipassana*).

4. The term *Sambodhi* used here refers to the phrase *Anuttara-samyak-sambodhi*,the highest form of wisdom joined with compassion. The phrase is found in the *Heart Sutra*, a brief chant used daily by all practitioners of Mahayana. The text is found in the appendix.

5. There are three kinds of Samatha "stop" practices described in this passage, i.e., thoughts on Basic substance, judging external causes, (here), and desisting from dispute. See Sekiguchi, p. 135.

6. See note 2 above, the second of the Three Wisdoms.

7. Zhiyi here explains the Middle Way, i.e., the Madhyamika school of meditation as the basis of *Samatha Vipasyana.* True compassion and wisdom arise from focusing on the "center" in the belly.

8. This last section does not necessarily belong to the original text of Zhiyi. It relates *Samatha Vipasyana* to the entire Buddhist tradition. Each sentence of the Chinese text is repeated twice as an introduction to the next idea. The repetitive phrase is left out of the translation.

9. A quote from the Lotus Sutra. See Sekiguchi, p. 136, footnote.

10. The ability to know clearly others thoughts, spiritual potencies, destinies; and protect from evil. See Inagaki, p. 328.

11. Mahayana Buddhism of China, Tantric Buddhism of Tibet and Japan teach that the Buddha has three bodily manifestations, i.e., the historical Buddha Sakyamuni, the Bodhisattva (who vows to save all sentient beings before going to the "other shore"), and the transformed or transcendent Buddha who has crossed over to the shore of eternity, and assists sentient beings by thelight of faith. These three "bodies" are called the *Dharmakaya* (Jpn. *Hosshin*, Chn. *Fashen*) Dharma

Body, the *Sambhogakaya* (Jpn. *Hojin*, Chn. *Baoshen*) Reward Body, and the *Nirmanakaya* (Jpn. *Keshin*, Chn. *Huashen*) Transformed Body.

12. Here the correct practice and achievements of "Stop" Look" Zen meditation are related to the Pure Land Buddhist school, which teaches that upon death the soul of the deceased goes first to a pleasant "Pure Land," from whence crossing to the eternal shore can be completed.

13. The Tathagata body includes the three kinds of Buddha, the Dharmakaya (wisdom and compassionate deeds), the Sambhogakaya (incarnate Bodhisattva, limitless compassion), and the Nirmanakaya of the Transcendent Buddha.

14. A story from the *Lotus Sutra*, the *Puo Da Duo* Chapter, tells how Nagakanya, daughter of the Dragon King, when eight years old achieved enlightenment from the Buddha.

THE HEART SUTRA

(Recited before and after Zen meditation)

When Avalokitesvara was walking on the shore of deep wisdom, enlightened, s/he saw that the five skandhas were completely empty, and thereupon crossed over all sorrow and care. "O Sariputra, form is not distinct from the empty, the empty is not distinct from form. Form is empty, emptiness is form. Sensation, imagination, judgement, consciousness too, empty. Sariputra, all Dharmas (thoughts) are empty of relation to Reality, i.e., They are not born or destroyed, not sullied or pure, not increased or diminished. The reason is because the empty (center) has no form, no sensation, imagination, judgment, or consciousness, no eyes, ears, nose, tongue, body feelings or mind thoughts, no color, sound, smell, taste, movement, object of thought, no world to see, no world to conceive or understand. No *avidya* ignorance and no end to ignorance. No old age and death, no escaping old age and death. No four noble truths (suffering, desire, cessation, path), no wisdom, nothing attained. Because nothing is attained, The enlightened rely on the shore of wisdom, and have no snares or obstacles. Free from snares, he/she has no fears. Freed from the world of dream images, at last he/she reaches Nirvana! All Buddhas of the Three Time Periods (past, now, future), rely on Wisdom's shore to attain unsurpassed, complete awakening. Therefore realize that the Wisdom Shore is a great spirit mantra, a great bright light mantra, a supreme, unequaled mantra, which can remove all suffering, a true, not false achievement. Therefore let us chant the Wisdom Shore Mantra! It goes like this:

Gone, gone, gone to the other shore! Arrived at the other shore.
Enlightened! Svaha!

Glossary:

Avalokitesvara = myself, filled with compassion;
Sariputra = myself, filled with wisdom.
Skandha = the five aggregates: form, perception, concept, volition, consciousness.
Buddhas = saints, people who respect and love others.
Mantra = a prayer to be recited vocally.
The other shore = wisdom joined with compassion. *Svaha* = Amen

SELECT BIBLIOGRAPHY

Abe, Masao, *Zen and Western Thought*, Ed. by W. R. LaFleur, Honolulu: 1985

Donner, N., Stevenson, D., *The Greater Calming & Contemplation Treatise*. Honolulu: 1993.

Dumoulin, H., Zen Buddhism, A History, 2 volumes, New York: 1988, 1990.

Enomiya-Lasalle, H., *Zen, Way to Enlightenment,* New York: 1966.

Inagaki, Hisao, *A Dictionary of Japanese Buddhist Terms*,* Kyoto:, 1988.

Iwano, Shinyu, *A Japanese-English Buddhist Dictionary*,* Tokyo: 1965.

Kapleau, P., *Three Pillars of Zen*, Tokyo: 1965.

Kasulis, T.P., *Zen Action - Zen Person*, Honolulu: 1981

Klein, Ann, *Knowledge and Liberation*, Ithaca: Snow Lion Publications, 1986.

Ku, Y.H., *History of Zen*, Pennsylvania: 1979.

Lai, W., & Lancaster, L., *Early Chan in China and Tibet*, Berkeley: 1983.

Hoffman, Yoel, (trans), *The Sound of One Hand*, New York: 1975.

Humphreys, C., *Zen Buddhism*, London: 1949.

Miura Isshu, Sasaki, R.F., *The Zen Koan*, Kyoto: 1965.

Saso, Michael, *Tantric Art and Meditation*, Honolulu: 1990.

Sekiguchi, S., *Tendai Shoshikan*,* Tokyo: 1978, 1991.

Suzuki, D.T., *An Introduction to Zen Buddhism*, New York: 1965.

___________, *The Training of the Zen Buddhist Monk*, Kyoto: 1934.

___________, *Zen and Japanese Cuilture*, Princeton: 1959.

Waldenfels, H., Absolute Nothingness: Foundations for Buddhist-Christian Dialogue, Translated by J.W. Heisig, New York: 1960.

Yampolski, Ph., *The Zen Master Hakuin*, New York-London: 1971.

Zhi Yi, *Xiuxi Zhiguan Zuo Chan Fayao*, Taisho Canon,* Vol. 46, No. 1915.

*texts of the Xiao Zhiguan, and the dictionaries used to translate.

Apartheid St

MEMORIES OF A POLITICAL PRISONER

Chengiah Rogers Ragaven

"How do you ban a human being? Home arrest, detention, exile, and assassination - all to silence, all to erase. Chengiah's "Memories of a Political Prisoner" is a declaration that the innate desire for freedom that burns in those who struggle against oppressive regimes is ultimately louder than the regime of silence. But "Memories of a Political Prisoner" is not triumphant, for Chengiah is aware that in the South Africa of today the chains of apartheid have been broken but the tools refurbished in neo-apartheid. This is a record, a reminder, and a warning that paradoxically is also a poetic celebration of the human spirit and the struggles to keep it alive."

- Mukoma Wa Ngugi, author of "Hurling Words at Consciousness" (AWP, 2006) and "Nairobi Heat" (Penguin Books SA, 2009

Dedication

This book is dedicated to my beloved parents Dorry and Chandramma Ragaven, my sister Marjorie Ragaven-Maistry, brothers Sonny, Lawrence, Niny, and Betsy who unstintingly shouldered "the pain, tribulations, and terror" of those difficult times. It is also dedicated to the wonderful people who lived in Reunion, especially in Ally Road, who were in fact our larger family in the village. Your support in those times will never be forgotten.

Acknowledgments

I want to express my thanks and appreciation to my wife Laurel, son Avi and daughter Samara who over the years have provided warmth and comfort as a family. My deep appreciation also goes to our graphic artist and friend, Christian Ayala, for his generous time and extraordinary skills.

Contents

Preface

When my father first asked me to write his preface, of course I was honored but above all I was confused. Why would one of the most intelligent, experienced and sometimes idolized persons ask me, a twenty year old "consumerist" girl mid-way through a college degree but somewhat lost, to write the very first few pages that the reader would see. So, having the relationship that I do with my father, I simply asked him. He calmly responded *because this Sumsa will inspire you to engage in Humanitarian and political work.* I balked at his words and since I hardly believe in my writing capabilities, was shocked that someone of his academic stature did.

After getting over some initial surprise and reading the pages written that would comprise this memoir, I realized that this book, these stories as much as they are about Chengiah Ragaven, are really about everyone who picks this book up to read it. Each part of his biography is for somebody. The preface for me, the introduction to Thomas Pooniah, the stories about Isipingo for his sister Margerie and for the parents that he never got to bury. The rest of the little anecdotes whether happy or sad, jubilant or tragic, scary or funny, are meant to inspire and entertain the person whose fingerprints feather across the white pages. And in some ways how very much like my father to make a book about him for other people, because that is what he has been doing his entire life. His service, time, passions have all been in efforts to give hope, freedom and happiness to everyone around him.

His biggest dedication has been to his home country of South Africa. From starting and ending the struggle against Apartheid, to the horrible aftermath when the country was trying to pick up the pieces of a broken regime. He risked his life and his family in order to stop the injustices that were blindly staring everyone is the face. At a time when very few other countries let alone people saw the hatred which emerged as a consequence of racism and segregation, my father stood up for the millions of Africans, Indians and Coloreds who comprised the majority in South Africa in numbers but the minority of voices heard.

But even his smaller projects are worth deserved praise, because they show that wherever he is, he will try to touch the lives of everyone around him. Moving to West Hartford, Connecticut, a place that outwardly seems like a little slice of utopia --tucked away with our manicured lawns, big cars, big smiles, "student of the month" children and big pay checks--who could need any help here, in middle class heaven? Only my father could see that behind all of this stay-at-home mothers were frustrated with using their Ivy League University degrees to figure out how to get Bobby to soccer practice while still getting Suzy on time to her ballet lesson.

That is how the American Womens International, a Solidarity movement with women abused worldwide on Middlefield Drive started. Where once a week my father had the entire mom community on our block over for curry and rice at our kitchen table.
From a personal viewpoint, it also seemed that ever since I was young my own peers have been drawn to my dad. Often the first thing my friends would ask when they came over was "Is your dad home?" because often he would take them into his little magnificent study where books reached the ceiling and littered the floor, and spin his tales capturing them with his wit and low unfamiliar accent.

He has always pushed me to be the best and moral person I can be and others have agreed that his optimism and unlimited love do the same for them. My whole life I have been told the stories that are in this book (and some I am still surprised to read), but to now know that everyone has access to these is the best feeling in the world and we as readers and bystanders should treasure each page of the magnificent manuscript.

But over all I hope that this book inspires you, the reader, to if not be a better person than to at least become aware of us as humans are capable of doing not for ourselves but for the humanity out there.

Shanthi Samara Ragaven
Smith College
Mass.USA

October 12, 2009

Chengiah Ragaven: Our Historical Role
By Thomas Ponniah

I have known Chengiah Ragaven since 1989. That year I was traveling around Europe, reading Hegel, and above all reflecting on my future: what role was I to play in the world around me? By the time I returned home to Montreal, I had decided that my education in political philosophy only had value if used to transform the world. Like most people who perceive oppression, I did not want to get involved in a confrontation with the authorities regarding social change; however my summer in Europe, amidst the fall of the Soviet Union and the emergence of civil society movements, changed my self-perception: that summer I realized that the nobility I associated with political philosophy only had depth if one was an agent of liberation, and not simply its spectator.

There is a saying: "when the student is ready, the teacher will appear". At the end of the summer of 1989, when I returned from Europe, I was ready for a political mentor. Within a week of returning a friend of mine, told me about an upcoming African solidarity event; he had been asked to be part of the organizing committee and he suggested that I also attend. I came to the meeting, met Chengiah, was impressed by him, and thus helped organize the event. Soon after under Chengiah's tutelage, the group of us started a new organization called "The ANC Solidarity Committee": this association began organizing talks, fundraisers and social events to raise awareness about the struggle against South African apartheid. At each one of our events Chengiah gave great, moving speeches about the demand that had been placed upon us: "two thirds of the world lives in poverty and it is your generation's historical role to support the liberation of that two thirds!" This was of course not the common thing one heard at the university; academics often focus their life's work on refining

concepts. The idea that an intellectual vocation was principled, romantic, and adventurous was something that I had never seen so thoroughly embodied before I met Chengiah. Professor Ragaven was worldly: he had been raised a Hindu, become active in radical student politics, been exiled from South Africa, went on to study at Oxford, and was now the most popular professor at Concordia University in Montreal, Canada. He was uncompromisingly committed to all of the great social mobilizations of the time: feminism, socialism, environmentalism, and of course the
greatest movement of the era, the struggle against apartheid. He brought all of his experience together in speeches that were fiery, compassionate, and eloquent. His presence hearkened us back to an era when revolution, in its noblest sense, was the driving principle of the Left.

Chengiah was not only a dazzling orator on the street but also one within the classroom: as a teacher he taught that institutions are not simply organizations made up of a set of stable roles; in fact these roles, or functions, are organized hierarchically and therefore some have more power to shape, to define and to intervene, than others. Chengiah, like many of the great radicals of the past, however was not content with simply defining institutions or uncovering their asymetrical relations. He, like his own political hero, Che Guevara, believed that an intellectual had to go beyond just interpreting reality. No, the purpose for an intellectual was to use knowledge to build another, better world.

Chengiah's commitment to a new, truly global society was demonstrated by his allegiance to alternatives: I heard Chengiah give speeches not only against various forms of oppression, but also for liberation. The defining theme of all the speeches was the call for freedom, freedom not only in its redistributive sense but also in its cultural, cognitive sense. The imagination had to also be set free: revolution was not simply a material transformation but also a mental one. All of his interventions, political organizing, and personal counsel shaped his fellow activists' consciousness of what the purpose of life should be, of what one's existence should express, and how one could participate in the advance human progress.

Chengiah has been and continues to be a great inspiration to young activists; he is one of the great sixties' activists who has kept utopian aspiration alive over the last generation. As conservatives transformed the word "revolution" into a term to describe technical innovation, militants like Chengiah have preserved the substantive meaning of the term. Today, with the growth of movements like the World Social Forum process, the anti-war movement, the new environmentalism, and numerous other activist projects, we can discern the emergence of a new cycle of global justice activism. And once again, at the front of the march, with his usual fire stands Chengiah, exhorting us to take account of the possibility that history has placed before us.

Dr. Thomas Ponniah is a Lecturer on Social Studies at Harvard University.
He is the co-editor of *Another World is Possible: popular alternatives to globalization at the World Social Forum.*

TO: CHENGIAH RAGAVEN @ ROGERS
(I.N. 800/481986A),
37 ALLY ROAD,
ISIPINGO RAIL,
DISTRICT OF DURBAN.

NOTICE IN TERMS OF SUB-SECTION (1) OF SECTION NINE OF THE SUPPRESSION OF COMMUNISM ACT, 1950 (ACT NO. 44 OF 1950).

WHEREAS I, PETRUS CORNELIUS PELSER, Minister of Justice, am satisfied that you engage in activities which are furthering or are calculated to further the achievement of any of the objects of communism, I hereby, in terms of sub-section (1) of section nine of the Suppression of Communism Act, 1950 (Act No. 44 of 1950), prohibit you for a period commencing on the date on which this notice is delivered or tendered to you and expiring on the **30th** day of **November** , 19**72** , from attending within the Republic of South Africa or the territory of South-West Africa -

(1) any gathering contemplated in paragraph (a) of the said sub-section; or

(2) any gathering contemplated in paragraph (b) of the said sub-section, of the nature, class or kind set out below:

(a) Any social gathering, that is to say, any gathering at which the persons present

/2...

MEMORIES OF A POLITICAL PRISONER

South African Political Prisoner No. I.N. 800/481986A

Wearing the mantle of a refugee and languishing in exile for over a quarter century, in a strange country where customs and traditions were so different from my people, fragmented memories of the warm and hospitable native land often flash through my mind. It is only those memories which kept me alive and I think sometimes, sane. For what use are the splendors of this world -- the pomp, glitter and power -- if the hearth, home and fireside of your ancestors cease to exist? Is that too much to ask?
Time, the chroniclers tell us, is the healer, and so the mind soon begins to adjust somewhat reluctantly and hazily to the present reality, but it fails however to halt the repetitious and continuously nagging memories of home, especially those weeklong village festivals and celebrations. Like an unforgettable dream it haunts the mind. Gushing memories of the sound of rhythmic drums and cymbals played by Minchee and Chinoda, sometimes swaying to the flute music and nadasuran of Thumbee who trails and follows the pagoda-like chariots honoring of the village Goddess – Mariamma. The throngs of multi-colored gaily-dressed peasant nymph- like extraordinarily beautiful women, dancing at festivals with their rustic styles and spontaneous warmth forces me to occupy my waking hours of the day. How does one forget the raucous laughter of youthful revelers at dusk, returning "sparked" from a party or the local bar, laughing and cajoling each other, now standing to debate a 'logic less' argument so common with drunken men. Then the familiar sounds of that extraordinary music, the sarangi and the doluck, and most of all the singing nightingales- these beautiful village maidens unique in so many ways, utter the sirenline songs- angelic in time, space and culture. And above all, how can one ever forget the sensuous and wafting smells of curries, masalas and spices, especially the biryani - that royal dish of the Mogul dynasty which has contributed so much to the exotic class of Indian cuisine? How I long to erase these memories, for they torture the soul and unhinge the mind. That, of course is

also have social intercourse with one another;

(b) any political gathering, that is to say any gathering at which any form of State or any principle or policy of the Government of a State is propagated, defended, attacked, criticised or discussed;

(c) any gathering of pupils or students assembled for the purpose of being instructed, trained or addressed by you.

Given under my hand at Pretoria on this 4th day of December, 1967.

MINISTER OF JUSTICE.

NOTE.

The Magistrate, Durban, has in terms of section 9(1) of the abovementioned Act been empowered to authorise exceptions to the prohibitions contained in this notice.

rather a difficult thing to do, for it seems that these memories are intertwined with fate and destiny, and are known to drive them unseen. My mind though, through some mysterious power, which I find difficult to rationalize, let alone think out, continuously reminds me of a particular time, of the past. In fact it is one summer day, an African summer day to be exact, in the tumultuous sixties, politically and or otherwise, when there was a sudden downpour of heavy rain most unexpectedly, with the pelting oblique crystal raindrops, accompanied by swivel-type gushing winds and occasional flashes of lightning with distant sounds of rumbling thunder.

"Oh my God!" I think. "Is that not the Greek god of thunder Thor, and the fire god Agni, who did not leave this earth as the myth would have us believe and is here in South Africa, well and alive?" That aside, this entire metaphysical 'nature experience'; aside from its sensual and aesthetic feelings undoubtedly, sounded like a philharmonic orchestra of the heavens, especially to the marshy dwellers of this village outpost of Reunion, near the Indian Ocean on the south coast of South Africa.

These marshlands are known to border the vast undulating British sugar plantations on the coastal belt of Natal. On this day, the wind, rain and lightning played music with their melodies on the million, swaying, wavy green razor-like thin leaves of the sugar cane plantation and created a movement that would be the envy of the Bolshoi Ballet. It was around here that most of the early indentured 'Mandradhi coolie' workers from South India settled, and who, through sheer endurance and torturous labor, transformed the craggy marshes and untamed lands, and established a thriving village. Three generations of slave labor, it is chronicled, turned this plantation outpost into a settlement. The Bristish plantation owners and their overseers, of course, with their experience of similar experiments of such cheap labor practices in other parts of the world, allowed the plantation workers, as part of their contract, either to return to India or to buy pieces of land on the marshland borders of the plantations. The long term objective of the sugar barons, it later became clear, was that in doing so they were

TO: CHENGIAH RAGAVEN @ ROGERS
(I.N. 800/481986A),
37 ALLY ROAD,
ISIPINGO RAIL,
DISTRICT OF DURBAN.

NOTICE IN TERMS OF SUB-SECTION (1) OF SECTION TEN QUAT OF THE SUPPRESSION OF COMMUNISM ACT, 1950 (ACT NO. 44 OF 1950).

WHEREAS there is in force against you a prohibition under sub-section (1) of section nine of the Suppression of Communism Act, 1950 (Act No. 44 of 1950), by way of a notice addressed and delivered or tendered to you, I, PETRUS CORNELIUS PELSER, Minister of Justice, hereby, in terms of sub-section (1) of section ten quat of the said Act, order you for a period commencing on the date on which this notice is delivered or tendered to you and expiring on the 30th day of **November**, 19**72**, to report to the officer in charge of the **Isipingo Police Station, Durban,** on every **Monday and Friday** between the hours of **seven** in the forenoon and **five** in the afternoon: **Provided that this notice shall not apply with reference to public holidays.**

Given under my hand at Pretoria on this 4th day of December, 1967.

MINISTER OF JUSTICE.

assured of continuous cheap labor close to the plantations for the expanding economy of the British Empire, and thereby guarantee for the future, cheap and efficient workforce for the extremely lucrative sugar industry for the colonialists in Africa.

What, at a cursory glance might seem, a sleepy windswept village of derelict corrugated iron shacks, all irregularly constructed and painted with the colors of the rainbow, one would, on closer view, see that it was made up of crisscross sandy pathways among worn out grassy patches of a sometimes lawn, interspersed with unimaginable spray of African ivy bushes with wild blood- red sun drenched flowers. The area was also noted for its tall, majestic wild branched syringa berry trees, with its sprays of purple and deep violet blossoms, the smells of which 'was perfume from paradise' in the air, spraying the entire village during summer with an odd palm tree here and there. Untold numbers of green leafed mango and wild banana trees grew in almost every backyard.

The average temperature on the coastal belt of Natal was renowned for its 72 degree temperature, although some days were extremely hot and humid. The village itself was constantly bathed with yellow sunlight, almost the whole year around, and the gentle breeze from the nearby Indian Ocean gently fluttered the evergreen leaves of the lush bushes with its tropical and Mediterranean trees surrounding the simple squatter-type settlement of the peasant folks. Should a stranger perhaps come to the village, it would not be uncommon to find the local women dressed in colorful saris and young maidens in floral dresses or sarongs going about their daily chores, for this area was designated "Indian" by the English colonialists long before the Apartheid system was established. The ladies adhered to a traditional old custom of friendliness, informality and near neighborliness, with a ready and wholesome smile and titillating laughter.

On this particular day, the sudden storm of that afternoon had caught them totally unawares. The stay at home mothers were seen running hither and thither, trying to take the half-dried clothes off the wire lines. These were a makeshift designed necessity, where two old bamboo poles were driven into the ground supported with chips of wood or iron and a thin wire or strong hemp rope were tied to the poles on the ends of either sides. They were competing

TO: CHENGIAH RAGAVEN @ ROGERS
(I.N. 800/481986A),
37 ALLY ROAD,
ISIPINGO RAIL,
DISTRICT OF DURBAN.

NOTICE IN TERMS OF PARAGRAPH (a) OF SUB-SECTION (1) OF SECTION TEN OF THE SUPPRESSION OF COMMUNISM ACT, 1950 (ACT NO. 44 OF 1950).

WHEREAS I, PETRUS CORNELIUS PELSER, Minister of Justice, am satisfied that you engage in activities which are furthering or may further the achievement of the objects of communism, I hereby, in terms of paragraph (a) of sub-section (1) of section ten of the Suppression of Communism Act, 1950 (Act No. 44 of 1950), prohibit you for a period commencing on the date on which this notice is delivered or tendered to you and expiring on the 30th day of November , 1972 , from -

(1) absenting yourself from -

(a) the residential premises situate at
37 Ally Road, Isipingo Rail, Durban,

at any time except -

(i) between the hours of six in the forenoon and six in the afternoon on any day not being a Saturday, Sunday or public holiday;

(ii) between the hours of six in the forenoon and two in the afternoon on any Saturday not being a public holiday;

2/...

20/

in fact, to beat the gushing wind-driven rain, pelting down on the village with the winds playing havoc mercilessly on the villagers. Amid the yelling at the kids to get into the houses there was much confusion, with the dogs barking and howling, drowning out the noise of the little children engaged in various ball games. They too soon begin to shout at each other or at those who were scampering for shelter, climbing trees and still others running around pushing their rusty bicycle wheels, which were stripped off their tires and pushed by means of a short stick in front of them, in order to 'park' them under trees for some protection from the rain.

"Angalaben, what are you cooking for supper tonight?" Samantha tried to enquire in between the intervening sounds, with her neighbor in the next yard, unpegging her husband's jaded and heavily patched shirt. 'Ben' was in fact a mark of respect and a shortened form for 'Bunie,' meaning 'sister' in Hindi.

"Fish curry," shouted Angalee, with the rain pelting on her face and half-wet with the heavy raindrops. "Bhai and Bechan went out early this morning to Reunion Rocks just before going to the factory. They caught six red snappers and we gave Santosh and Jamila two of the bigger fishes. They are so poor, you know, and the husband now works short time. How they survive I don't know but I am sure the in-laws who are rather poor themselves help them out now and then!"

By now, the thunder, lightning and rain were coming down in showers and woman ran to their respective houses, clutching their half-wet clothes.

Ally Road, the main 'thoroughfare ' of the village was really a pathway, named after "Professor" Ally. He had become famous in those times not as some learned man in the usual sense of the word but as a village magician extraordinaire, and who had become a national icon, even in the days of apartheid. So extraordinary was his skills, rare for an Indian at that but also because of his very Arabian styled fashion- exotic, charming with an all consuming smile, with a gray beard and a turban, completed the mystique, conjuring up all kinds of tricks of the Arabian Nights. Dressed in his black suit and bow tie and always with a charming smile with a gold tooth, he was the first from the village

(b) the magisterial district of **Durban**;

(2) being within -

(a) any Bantu area, that is to say -

(i) any location, Bantu hostel or Bantu village defined and set apart under the Bantu (Urban Areas) Consolidation Act, 1945 (Act No. 25 of 1945);

(ii) any area approved for the residence of Bantu in terms of section 9(2)(h) of the Bantu (Urban Areas) Consolidation Act, 1945 (Act No. 25 of 1945);

(iii) any Scheduled Bantu Area as defined in the Bantu Land Act, 1913 (Act No. 27 of 1913);

(iv) any Bantu Township established under the Regulations for the Administration and Control of Townships in Bantu Areas, promulgated in Proclamation No. R.293 of the 16th November, 1962;

(v) any land of which the South African Bantu Trust, referred to in section 4 of the Bantu Trust and Land Act, 1936 (Act No. 18 of 1936), is the registered owner or any land held in trust for a Bantu Tribal Community in terms of the said Bantu Trust and Land Act, 1936;

3/...

to travel with his troupe around the country as a magician. He was an impressive figure, both off and on the stage, and brought great honor to the village folk. The socialite brothers of the 'Professor', Ebrahim, and Mubaruk "Lighty" Ally, were also greatly respected by the villagers, as were their families. Added to this was the fact as Muslims who otherwise were mainly merchants and rich and considered themselves a class above the local villagers added to their prestige.
The road could hardly be called that for it was a sandy gravel path, which bordered the village on the western side and ran parallel to the elevated railway tracks on the East. The 'Banana Express' the 'pride' of the South African railway system with its puffing steam engine from Port Shepstone to Durban Central was the favorite train on this route, although the commuter train taking workers to the industrial surrounding areas ran every hour during the peak periods of the day. Two or three times a day the never-ending goods train ran, indicating that South Africa was rapidly industrializing like all other colonial countries.
As mentioned elsewhere, the road was in name only. The local white council had, long before the Apartheid system was established, an extension of the British colonial government political machinery with its entrenched racial mandate. The Europeans in Natal, considered as the 'last outpost' of white supremacy, had always been wholly unobservant and negligent of their civic responsibilities towards their 'non-European people.' This was in spite of the heavy taxation levied on these peasants. As a result, Ally Road was really an overgrown path, widened by the occasional heavy-duty municipal service truck, but used by the villagers as a regular road. The potholes and gullies caused through the heavy floods were filled with rubble by the village people themselves. Cars, however were a rare sight on this road and therefore when a large black Ford Sedan was seen driving slowly on the pathway, it was obvious to the villagers that it must be making its way to the Ragaven house.
The time of November to these simple villagers had always been a month of anticipation. For them, it was the month before the Christmas holidays, the most anticipated time of the year, a period of expectation, of the soon-to-come meager bonuses to buy

(b) any Bantu compound;

(c) the premises of any factory as defined in the Factories, Machinery and Building Work Act, 1941 (Act No. 22 of 1941);

(d) any place which constitutes the premises on which any publication as defined in the Suppression of Communism Act, 1950, is prepared, compiled, printed or published;

(e) any place which constitutes the premises of any organization contemplated in Government Notice No. R.2130 of the 28th December, 1962, as amended by Government Notice No. R.1947 of the 27th November, 1964, and any place which constitutes premises on which the premises of any such organization are situate;

(f) any place or area which constitutes the premises on which any public or private university, university college, college, school or other educational institution is situate, except until the 31st January, 1968, the premises of the University of Natal, Durban;

(g) any place or area which constitutes the premises of any superior or inferior court as defined in the Criminal Procedure Act, 1955 (Act No. 56 of 1955), except for the purpose of -

(i) applying to a magistrate for an exception to any prohibition in force against you under the Suppression of Communism Act, 1950;

(ii) attending any criminal proceedings in which you are required to appear as an accused or a witness;

(iii) attending any civil proceedings in which you are a plaintiff, petitioner, applicant, defendant, respondent or other party or in which you are required to appear as a witness;

../

presents and food, plan for gaiety and fun, and finally, get a rest from the daily grind of work. In colonial countries, the foreign-owned factories are still reminiscent of Coketown; Charles Dickens famous picture of grinding labor and smoke bellowing chimneys. Poor folks, as a rule, around the world looked forward to festivals and holidays for the fun and joy in life, for a respite from the exacting labor on land and the harsh industrial systems that extract every ounce of sweat and blood from its colonial vassals. It was on one of these November days, the exact date, still being in doubt among the villagers and factory workers, although firmly etched in his memory, when Neerputh, returning from Isipingo Beach with his bare feet, wearing his salt-wet, oversized patched pants with fishing rods (from which dangled three red snappers) resting on his shoulders, as fishermen in this part of the world are in the habit of carrying their tools of trade, thought he heard water splash behind him. When he turned around, he caught a glimpse of the slow cruising black Ford.

Neerputh and Muntoon, father and son, were drunk as usual, swaying from one side of the path to the other. How they negotiated the innumerable puddles on the roads, positioning their feet on the stones that were placed to cross over, was always a puzzle to the local residents. The path came to an abrupt end at the end of the bridge, only to continue on the other side. The narrow bridge close to the Bandhwa's house itself was a masterpiece of engineering undertaken by ordinary folks. It was not completely washed away during the heavy summer floods as the other bridges, only because of the prompt and expert repairs carried out by local volunteers. Therefore, the existing bamboo frame and corrugated iron, the 'steel technology' of the bridge, unorthodox in its construction in many places would have insulted many an engineer, but they never the less will be forced to concede that this 'third world engineering' must be complimented, for it was never known to collapse like other government structures around the area, in spite of the constant floods.

The sedan now cruised along and stopped near a rather large pool of muddy water immediately under the overhanging mango trees that grew in abundance in the area. In the meantime Neerputh was

(h) **any harbour as defined in section one of the Railways and Harbours Control and Management (Consolidation) Act, 1957 (Act No. 70 of 1957);**

(3) communicating in any manner whatsoever with any person whose name appears on any list in the custody of the officer referred to in section eight of the Suppression of Communism Act, 1950, or in respect of whom any prohibition under the Suppression of Communism Act, 1950, or the Riotous Assemblies Act, 1956 (Act No. 17 of 1956), is in force ;

(4) performing any of the following acts, that is to say -

(a) preparing, compiling, printing, publishing, disseminating or transmitting in any manner whatsoever any publication as defined in the Suppression of Communism Act, 1950;

(b) participating or assisting in any manner whatsoever in the preparation, compilation, printing, publication, dissemination or transmission of any publication as so defined;

(c) contributing, preparing, compiling or transmitting in any manner whatsoever any matter for publication in any publication as so defined;

(d) assisting in any manner whatsoever in the preparation, compilation or transmission of any matter for publication in any publication as so defined;

5/...

trying to negotiate the stones placed in that very muddy pool, the trees now being on one side and the car on the other, when Sergeant Naiger, the notorious Indian Security Branch policeman who was known for his continuous persecution of Indian political activists, could be seen sitting in the back seat of the car. He wore a perpetual smile -- no, more of a smirk -- on his face.

"Ah! My fishermen friends!" he called out. Neerputh blinked for a moment, not sure where the call of his name had come from dazed as he was, which was his normal state of earthly existence. Two black suited men with military style haircuts sat in front of the car. It was all a bit hazy for him as usual, but how could he forget Naiger, who only two weeks before accosted him at the Deera, a makeshift tin shack on the beach used by the local fisherman for shelter?

"And how is fishing this morning?"

"Good, oh! I say good, Sergeant, the shad run has just begun, but this year we, we don't have money to repair. He stopped to straighten himself, "the nets," he stammered with a drunken slur.

"And your license is due to be renewed at the end of this month, as I remember."

"Yes! Sergeant, that is true."

"Well, keep in mind that there is work to be done before that is possible!" Neerputh had no idea what that was to mean, but he nodded and stammered yet again, "Yes, sir!"

"By the way, you know Dorry's son, don't you?"

It was obvious to the sergeant that these families went back in time when their grandparents arrived in the Truro from India, with a very different set of circumstances: rather like the North American slave trade from Africa instead of being compared with the people arriving on the Mayflower on the eastern coast of the United States, or settlers coming to Sydney harbor in Australia or anywhere else for that matter. For the people here, as for the rest of the victims of cultural genocide, one of the intended ingredients of capitalism's greed, was that this trade of commercial human cargoes and the dumping of human peoples means 'production of wealth' all over the British Empire, remains as fresh and perhaps more poignant than any one time incident in history, because it has been happening for centuries and continues routinely to this

(e) (i) preparing, compiling, printing, publishing, disseminating or transmitting in any manner whatsoever any document (which shall include any book, pamphlet, record, list, placard, poster, drawing, photograph or picture which is not a publication within the meaning of paragraph (4)(a) above); or

(ii) participating or assisting in any manner whatsoever in the preparation, compilation, printing, publication, dissemination or transmission of any such document,

in which, inter alia -

(aa) any form of State or any principle or policy of the Government of a State is propagated, defended, attacked, criticised, discussed or referred to;

(bb) any matter is contained concerning any body, organization, group or association of persons, institution, society or movement which has been declared an unlawful organization by or under the Suppression of Communism Act, 1950, or the Unlawful Organizations Act, 1960;

(cc) any matter is contained concerning any organization contemplated in Government Notice No. R.2130 of the 28th December, 1962, as amended by Government Notice No. R.1947 of the 27th November, 1964; or

6/...

present day. While the former whites came to these lands as masters, indentured plantation workers and slaves were brought to act as a fifth column support staff in this 'conquest land'. The wise Zulus did not yield to white pressure and were content to follow their ancient pastoral lifestyle, and enjoy the Indian Ocean coast, with its most exotic greenish blue waters as it lay untampered, which they discovered was the dream of every middle and upper class white, and they were not about ready to exchange this for white servitude. However, Dorry Ragaven no longer followed his father into the sugarcane slave labor market, but "diversified" into becoming a 'cook boy' for one of the various English families that followed the sugar entrepreneurs for the good life in Africa and the colonies. He was not alone, for each family had three or four servants to service the masters, one maid for the kitchen and bedrooms, and a garden boy to attend to the outside chores. Of course, these garden boys were fathers, even grandfathers in some cases of the Africans or Indians. That pain of racism and the cavalier treatment of people did not die with the generations of the past. The cultural pain, racial experiences and neurosis let alone social and economic immobility had left millions of non-whites as underclass even in this current generation with its collective memory.

The parents of Dorry and Neerputh were plantation workers together and lived in the village. Unlike old man Neerputh, his friend Dorry had gone to work in a factory downtown, while Neerputh drifted into becoming a local fisherman. In terms of caste he was a chamar, which regulated him to certain acceptable vocations, not that this meant anything in South Africa, but the older Hindus for some years adhered to the strong cultural traditions of the Motherland, which became diluted over the years when clashing with other newer forms of cultural liberation. The fishing community was mainly Hindi speaking and lived separately in the village, a section called 'Machiewala,' well known for its fishy smell, half-constructed boats, nets lying everywhere, and endless fishing rods made of the local bamboos at different stages of finishing. The huts and shanty dwellings of these fisher folk were unusually ill constructed with mud and bamboos wanting in various stages of repair.

(dd) any matter is contained which is likely to engender feelings of hostility between the White and the non-White inhabitants of the Republic of South Africa;

(f) giving any educational instruction in any manner or form to any person other than a person of whom you are a parent;

(g) taking part in any manner whatsoever in the activities or affairs of any organization contemplated in Government Notice No. R.2130 of the 28th December, 1962, as amended by Government Notice No. R.1947 of the 27th November, 1964;

(h) taking part in any manner whatsoever in the affairs or activities of any students' society or organization;

(5) receiving at the said residential premises any visitor other than a medical practitioner for medical attendance on you or members of your household, if the name of such medical practitioner does not appear on any list in the custody of the officer referred to in section <u>eight</u> of the Suppression of Communism Act, 1950, and no prohibition under the Suppression of Communism Act, 1950, or the Riotous Assemblies Act, 1956,

7/...

The sergeant was well aware that the fishermen in the village relied on Ken, the younger brother of Dorrie Ragaven, and the village schoolmaster for completing the application forms for fishing licenses. "I want you to keep an eye on the house," he continued, "and tell me about the people who come and go there, especially the movements of the university boy. I want all the information you can get, and by the way," he paused for a while, acting out his security police routine, "tell your friends to keep an eye open, too." The tone was all executed in the best Afrikaner police tradition and was done too to impress his masters in the front seat.

"Yes, sir," stammered Neerputh, again not realizing the full implication of the motives of the request paying more interest in getting his feet on the stones in the puddles and being totally inabrietated.

It was years later when he realized what this implied, but that was too late. Indirectly, he was being recruited to become a police informer and spy for the notorious "Security Branch," the National Security Agency of the Apartheid State, and was unknowingly in fact asked to become a collaborator and work for the State against the freedom struggle of South Africa, which in spirit he would never done.

The cane spirit, the favorite and highly intoxicating liquor of the poor Indian community, freed Neerputh and Muntoon temporarily of the 'incident' as they continued their walk, swaying side to side not only because they were in a drunken state, but also because to cross the puddles on slippery stones was a balancing act on its own. They stopped several times, to emphasize some point facing each other, or to exchange greetings of "Ram, Ram Bhai," (God be with you brothers) with some of their neighbors, for village dwellers are known to be friendly with each other, and, in fact, in this Reunion outpost, they constituted one large family by marriage, kinship or caste.

They stopped for a moment while lighting up their pieces of cigarettes, which Muntoon produced from his upper pocket as a brown paper-covered 'stompie,' the butt end of a cigarette. They then looked up to see Mr. Abdul Raimen, dressed in his usual is in force in respect of such medical practitioner.

Given under my hand at Pretoria on this 4th day of December, 1964.

MINISTER OF JUSTICE.

NOTE.

The Magistrate, Durban, has in terms of section 10(1)(a) of Act No. 44 of 1950 been empowered to authorise exceptions to the prohibitions contained in this notice.

gray pants and sports coat and a black Fez, turn into his pathway, which was perhaps the most neatly trimmed hedge way and garden anywhere in the village.

"Good afternoon, Mr. Abdul," they stammered.

"Good afternoon," replied Mr. Abdul politely. Neerputh turned to his son Muntoon. "That, my son, is a gentleman." Muntoon nodded his head in acquiescence, for in the village the Raimens were considered a model family since all their children were at College and this was unusually rare. As they merrily walked along, exchanging greetings with some and talking with others, the village became aware that the special police were on their way to harass the Ragaven family once again.

News and its interpretations within village communities followed their own dynamics. In this particular case of the security police operations, this community had little or no knowledge of their national security apparatus or the wider objectives of the white Apartheid state. It was generally understood that this young neighbor of theirs was a follower of Chief Albert Luthuli, the head of the African National Congress, and must be implicated in some serious anti-government political activity beyond their understanding. Politics in this country are generally regarded as a class activity, especially of the white upper class, and insofar as the general mass of ordinary people were concerned, newspapers fed them with the one-liner sensations usually accompanied by a large photograph of some politician making a statement unintelligible to anyone except for the initiated. The fact that one of their sons was fighting against the white oppressive government, they rationalized, lent extraordinary prestige and respect to this neighbor. Yet there were others who feared that anyone involved with the police for whatever reason must, by definition, be involved in some form of criminal act, but what kind they could not fathom, since the family was well respected in the village.

From the time that Neerputh and Muntoon had seen the black sedan they had reached Bundwha's Bridge, the sighting of the car and the tales woven around it had reached the sleepy village. Suddenly, the village was abuzz, recollecting the various past episodes of the Special Branch raids on the house, which occurred

TO: CHENGIAH RAGAVEN @ ROGERS
(I.N. 800/481986A),
37 ALLY ROAD,
ISIPINGO RAIL,
DISTRICT OF DURBAN.

NOTICE IN TERMS OF SUB-SECTION (1) OF SECTION NINE OF THE SUPPRESSION OF COMMUNISM ACT, 1950 (ACT NO. 44 OF 1950).

WHEREAS I, PETRUS CORNELIUS PELSER, Minister of Justice, am satisfied that you engage in activities which are furthering or are calculated to further the achievement of any of the objects of communism, I hereby, in terms of sub-section (1) of section nine of the Suppression of Communism Act, 1950 (Act No. 44 of 1950), prohibit you for a period commencing on the date on which this notice is delivered or tendered to you and expiring on the 30th day of November , 19 72 , from attending within the Republic of South Africa or the territory of South-West Africa -

(1) any gathering contemplated in paragraph (a) of the said sub-section; or

(2) any gathering contemplated in paragraph (b) of the said sub-section, of the nature, class or kind set out below:

(a) Any social gathering, that is to say, any gathering at which the persons present

/2...

sometimes late at night and at other times in the early hours of the morning. The detentions and continual harassment of the young man were recounted, including the pressure put on certain members of the village community to act as spies and informers. Although all of these incidents were interpreted personally, others recognized the larger landscape of it as being a part of the liberation struggle that was unfolding within the country -- the imprisonment of Nelson Mandela, the banning of the ANC and the PAC, people escaping into exile, and the rise of peoples political consciousness in the country. Some recounted how Steve Biko, Ben Ngubane, Thami Mhalimbiso, Asha Ntanga, Katie Abrahams or Darkie Sepopedi was often seen with other young political leaders at this village house of the Ragavens. Mystery, intrigue and myth, bonded with the fishermen's tales, reached a stature such that Michner or a John Gresham would have woven it into a popular novel.

Crossing this bridge required the ability of a rope balancing actor; an artist of sorts, so to speak, so that when the two fishermen, with their catch hanging precariously from their rods, with pants now utterly wet and muddy, oversized in the first place, had to step over various jutting rocks, some pointed and others rounded, with the roaring over-flooded river underneath- this Scylla and Charybdis maneuvering silenced even the breeze-blown grass on the banks, let alone the hushed audience of the few onlookers who gathered nearby to watch the act. Undoubtedly, the symphony of the gushing waters and the movement of these two men doing a balancing act was creating a perfect harmony for an operatic drama. What took minutes at the best of times looked like an eternity, and, when the last steps were taken, the assembled crowd hushed with expectation suddenly clapped and cheered with the children falling over themselves in imitating father and son.

The Bundwha children were standing on the verandah of the house, which bordered the stream. They clapped the loudest and shouted "Hurray!" and chuckled at the dexterity of the two older village folk with their fishing rods.

Hardly had they crossed the bridge when clambering down from the railway tracks, on a path leading down to the road from also have social intercourse with one another;

(b) any political gathering, that is to say any gathering at which any form of State or any principle or policy of the Government of a State is propagated, defended, attacked, criticised or discussed;

(c) any gathering of pupils or students assembled for the purpose of being instructed, trained or addressed by you.

Given under my hand at Pretoria on this 4th day of December, 1967.

MINISTER OF JUSTICE.

NOTE.

The Magistrate, **Durban**, has in terms of section 9(1) of the abovementioned Act been empowered to authorise exceptions to the prohibitions contained in this notice.

Jamadars Trading Store, which was on the other side of the tracks and on the main Reunion road, came the village-renowned maiden Sharika. Her exquisite beauty, it was rumored, was unparalleled in the glamour centers of the world, a statement made by a Hollywood film crew who came to the village a few years earlier to make a documentary on the sugar plantations in Natal. Barefoot with anklets, dressed in a Kalwar Shimiz of azure blue, her long black hair flowing in the wind, with a crimson dot on her forehead, and the shining nose ring on her right nostril: all of these features, along with her naturally entrancing smile, stopped the travelers upon sight of her, in spite of their drunkenness. “Namaste, uncles!” she called out. For it was custom in the village to address elders with respect. The fishermen mumbled their greetings, staring at this beautiful figure as she skipped through the narrow lanes and was soon out of sight to her humble tin-roofed house.

The security car in the meantime had driven around the bend and was now on the overgrown path leading to the political dissenter’s house. The driver, a Sergeant Stadler, veteran in the security agency, had the reputation of being a ruthless enforcer of the Apartheid laws. Both respected and feared at the Security Headquarters, he was known to enjoy his work immensely with Law and Order being his specialty. It was rumored among the security grapevine that he worshipped and was a great admirer of one Henry Kissinger from America.

His investigations into what were called “political offences,” and his rigorous pursuit of ‘troublemakers,’ as he labeled extra-parliamentary political activists, had enabled him to make rapid promotion within the police force. Always impeccably dressed in a black suit, white silk shirt and tie to match, not forgetting the tiepin; he resembled the South African ‘professional’ in the world of security. His thin moustache was the trademark of the security policeman. The National Security budget was by far the largest slice of all governmental spending, and as such, Sergeant Stadler was accustomed to the best that South Africa could offer her white community, and driving through Ally Road was not one of them. The potholes and the wide ditches that this marshy outpost of thc

J. 424.

Telegramadres: „LANDDROS."
Telegraphic Address: "MAGISTRATE."

Gelieve in u antwoord te verwys na
In reply please quote

No. 17/33/4/47

REPUBLIEK VAN SUID-AFRIKA.—REPUBLIC OF SOUTH AFRICA.

LANDDROSKANTOOR,
MAGISTRATE'S OFFICE,

PRIVATE BAG 4308,
DURBAN.

13th December, 1963.

Mr. Chengiah Ragaven @ Rogers,
Alley Road,
ISIPINGO.

Dear Sir,

SECTION 10(1)TER VAN WET NO. 44 VAN 1950.

You are required to call on the Chief Magistrate as soon as possible.

Yours faithfully,

MAGISTRATE : DURBAN.

JM.

Indian Bantustan was one of the hazards of this kind of job, but the Captain was always looking for challenges and he considered this one of them.

Finally, the car stopped on the pathway of the garden near the unfinished half-bricked steps, which remained unplastered in the midst of the terraces of the lawn. Blossoms of hydrangeas were on one side and azanias on the other. Bright red canners within triangles also decorated both sides, and a mango tree grew in the center. Betsy, one of a number of children playing in the backyard, heard a car door shut, peeked sideways, and saw the two white special branch men climbing up the stairs.

"Aka, Aka," he shouted, calling his sister in the vernacular. She was in the laundry yard of the house gathering the daily washings from the clotheslines erected with bamboos in the backyard. "There are two white men and I think there is an Indian man also walking behind them. They are coming up the stairs."

Marjorie intuitively knew that these must be Special Branch people and a shiver went up her spine. The routine intimidation had been a continuing pattern for many years; so much so, that the abhorrent racism routine in all aspects of daily life, which had rendered existence itself a burden for much of Black life, was in fact made intolerable by these intrusions. The fear of impending disaster, whatever it might be, crossed her mind. She hurriedly threw the gathered clothing into the basket on the grass with the pegs on top, undid her apron, and rushed through the passage to open the front door.

"Good afternoon, Miss," the sergeant said with his usual public relations plastic smile. "We have come to have a little chat with your brother!" The conversation was conducted with as much formality as there could be, for both sides knew the animosity the family harbored for the intrusions on their privacy over the many years. These very men, along with several others, had come and raided the house routinely, sometimes knocked down the front door, or otherwise jumped through the windows on being told that a meeting was being held, and were also known to prowl around the yard at all hours of the night and day. They had often dragged off the 'agitator,' 'communist,' 'troublemaker' ANC member,

01/172589
(Z. 14.)

REPUBLIEK VAN SUID-AFRIKA.  REPUBLIC OF SOUTH AFRICA.

Verw. Nr./Ref. No. 17/33/4/47

NAVRAE/ENQUIRIES:

Tel. No.

KANTOOR VAN DIE—OFFICE OF THE
MAGISTRATE,
PRIVATE BAG 4308,
DURBAN.

19th February, 1968.

Mr. C. Ragaven,
37 Ally Road,
ISIPINGO RAIL.

Dear Sir,

I regret to advise you that your application to enter the premises of the University of Natal for the purpose of enrolling as a full-time student is refused.

Yours faithfully,

MAGISTRATE : DURBAN

JM

at all hours of the night, for what they politely referred to as 'questioning.' Such were the tragedies of the liberation struggle in South Africa over several decades.

But Marjorie was not unmindful of the ancient Indian customs and culture of her traditions.

"Good afternoon," she replied. "Do please sit down. Can I get you something to drink? I will call my brother. He is with the neighbors."

The 'visitors' thanked her and politely refused the refreshments offered.

The neighbors in the meantime had noticed the car and seen the security policemen walk over to the house. These visits prompted fear and apprehension for neighbors, for in such communities of close networks; they would not be beyond the suspicion of collaborating or aiding and abetting 'agitators.' Such was the rationale endemic of the police state in South Africa. In the meantime, the 'victim' was already walking through the backyard fence over to his house when his sister informed him of the police.

"Now what," he thought to himself. A thousand thoughts raced through his mind. What crime would they now accuse him of? Or would they march him off for the usual protocol 'questioning,' a euphemism for bullying, threatening, torturing, and other gross violations of human rights, all legitimized in the name of the 'security of the state.' This unique human experience of political prisoners hardly appears in the compendium of psychological types in history, since it is the unique experience of small groups of humanity around the world who keep alive the moral integrity of civilizations. In this situation one dies a million deaths, but then who knows what the price for human freedom and dignity is? The family goes through their own traumas: the mother's anguish for a son or daughter detained, the father seeing his children abused, brothers and sisters at their various stages of love and compassion for their loved ones, and of course the neighbors and friends of this poor but lovable culture of solidarity and village folk collectively. If one could only hear the narratives of the indigenous peoples of the world: the peasants of the Banana Republics of Latin America, Vietnam, colonial Africa, the plantation folk of the Caribbean, the Jews of the holocaust, the Palestinians in Palestine, and, moreover,

P.O. Box 41,
ISIPINGO RAIL,
Natal.
17th Nov.,1968.

The Chief Magistrate,
Private Bag 4308,
DURBAN.

Dear Sir,

re: PERMISSION TO LEAVE MAGISTERIAL AREA OF DURBAN.

I have been served with Notice in terms of Sub Section (1) of section 9/ten and ten quat of the Suppression of Communism Act 1950 (Act No.44 of 1950).

On the 12th November, 1968 I was issued on application, a permit in terms of the Departure from the Union Regulation Act 1955.

I wish to leave Durban on Sunday the 24th November, 1968 proceeding to the United Kingdom and seek permission to leave my residence 37 Ally Road, Isipingo Rail, at 1 p.m. and then proceed to the Louis Botha Airport.

Please comment on the "gathering" aspect as will be applied before departure.

Yours sincerely,

C. RAGAVEN.

the below-the-breadline two-and-a-half-billion women, all being oppressed in the name of 'global democracy.' They too understand all too well this shared experience.
By the time he reached the lounge area, which was called the 'sitting room' in the so-called old days in this part of the world, he had recovered his composure and in his usual amiable style, greeted his visitors.
"Ah," said Sergeant Stadler, always the first to speak on such occasions. "You know Sergeant Naiger, and this is Captain Van Nie-Kirk." The Captain nodded with a knowing plastic smile, and going through his mind was the familiar phrase the Special Branch circles have: "Oh! This is that man I have heard so much about! Pity, I did not get my hands on him earlier!"
Of course, the Security Branch was well aware of their client. He certainly was not the average 'agitator.' Students in general, and especially student leaders, were a class of their own. Over the years the security establishment had studied the psychological profiles of revolutionary leadership in the country. The South African Intelligence community's strategy and tactics in intelligence gathering were beginning to become sophisticated, with the help of the CIA, MI6, and MOSSAD. One thing this 'brotherhood' had to admit was that the revolutionary leadership, young and old, could be trusted to be frank and forthright in all matters. Apart from the political secrets and revolutionary plans, whatever they might be, Africans here could be trusted to be forthright about their liberation struggle. The Branch itself admitted that the leadership possessed integrity. That was until the early sixties, at the time of the Sharpville massacre. In the aftermath of the sixties, with international condemnation, the fifth column of racist supporters arrived in South Africa to lend solidarity to the struggle, and the whole 'struggle-culture' was changing, especially with the infiltration of liberal international solidarity movements and NGO's were infiltrating the liberation movement. While there were some extraordinary, genuine individuals who understood the struggles of 'third world people' and were very committed to social, political, and economic change, there were others: various kinds of 'adventurers' and opportunists

01/72909
(L. 14)

REPUBLIEK VAN SUID-AFRIKA.  REPUBLIC OF SOUTH AFRICA.

Verw. Nr./Ref. No. 17/33/4/47

NAVRAE/ENQUIRIES.

Tel. No.

KANTOOR VAN DIE–OFFICE OF THE
Magistrate,
Durban.

18th November, 1968.

Mr. C. Ragaven,
P.O. Box 41,
ISIPINGO RAIL.

Dear Sir,

With reference to your letter of the 17th November, 1968, I have to inform you that as you have now been issued by the Secretary of the Interior with a permit in terms of the Departure from the Union Regulation Act, 1955, (Permit No. P.03407 dated 11th November, 1968), permission is hereby granted to you to leave the Magisterial district of Durban for the purpose of proceeding to the United Kingdom by air, subject to the following conditions :-

(a) That you depart from Louis Botha Airport by South African Airways aircraft scheduled to leave Louis Botha Airport at 2.40 p.m. on Sunday, 24th November, 1968 for Jan Smuts Airport;

(b) That you depart from Jan Smuts Airport by B.O.A.C. aircraft scheduled to leave that airport at 6 p.m. on Sunday, 24th November, 1968;

(c) That from the time of your arrival at until the time of your departure from Jan Smuts airport you remain within the Airport buildings.

The remaining conditions of the notice in terms of paragraph (a) of sub-section (1) of section ten of the Suppression of Communism Act, 1950 (Act No. 44 of 1950) which was served upon you remain of full force and effect.

Yours faithfully,

MAGISTRATE : DURBAN.

who 'played militancy' and were often on the payroll of 'foreign masters.' They were routinely 'planted' within liberation movements, with the sole aim of destabilizing the struggle for independence and freedom of the African peoples.
For now, they knew that this young student was the best among his peers. Sergeant Naiger had not forgotten a certain morning when he raided the young man's home at about four in the morning after a few pylons were blown near the Reunion International Airport, a few miles from the Ally Road House. He questioned the young man and accused him of being a communist. The unexpected, retort which caught the policeman unaware was, "Are you accusing me of being a Stalinist, Leninist, Maoist, Cuban, or a Ukrainian communist?" All of which confused the unschooled police official. The young intellectual concluded, "Please don't insult us -- our ideology goes much further than dominating systems of thought!" That proved too much for the security policeman, who thought it better not to engage him any further and concentrate his energy on the blowing up of the Pylons rather than in academic debate about the tenets and conjectured theories of the various strands of communism.
Still attempting to be pleasant, Captain Van Nie Kerk broke in with a wry plastic smile and calmly said, "We have an early Christmas present for you." And saying that, he reached out and opened up his black leather briefcase, took out what seemed a wad of typewritten sheets of paper, some stapled and others loose. As he handed over the papers, all three got up to leave.
Years later, if one tried to recapture this moment, it has always remained somewhat confused and unreal, and rather difficult to recount precisely the exact sequence of events. It all happened within a few moments, and then they were leaving through the front door. A feeling of numbness and unknowingness set in. I heard myself saying farewell as the visitors were leaving.
I remember throwing down the wad of papers on the sofa, walking out of the front door with them, and then turning right into a cutting through the fence back to my neighbor's house. The house remained tense until my brother, Niny, who always kept a watch, reported back to the family that all was well, that the police had

Our ref: TRR084109

Mr Chengiah Ragaven
16 Clairwood Road
Highlands Estate
Vredehoek

08 September 1998

Dear Mr Ragaven

Statement number(s): KZN/NG/250/DN

The Truth and Reconciliation Commission would like to thank you once again for having come forward to make a statement to us. We have received over 20 000 statements and more than 7 000 applications for amnesty.

The statements have been investigated, and we are now able to inform you that the Human Rights Violation Committee has found that a gross violation of human rights has occurred and is of the opinion that you are a victim thereof.

Now that this finding has been made, you may be eligible for reparation. If you wish to apply for such reparation, please complete the enclosed Reparations Application Form and send it to the Reparation and Rehabilitation Committee using the self addressed envelope.

Whether or not you decide to take up this opportunity, we want you to know that the recording of your experience has made a significant contribution to the work of the Truth and Reconciliation Commission. It helped us to understand the nature and the extent of the violations which took place. It will form a part of the permanent record which will remain for future generations. It has allowed us to fulfill our task of exposing the truth about what happened in the years of conflict.

The Final Report will be presented to the State President at the end of July 1998. The process of which your story has been a part has helped to lay the foundations for the reconciliation for which we must all work if we wish to secure a peaceful and stable future for South Africa.

We send you our thanks and our best wishes.

Yours sincerely,

Archbishop Desmond Mpilo Tutu (Chairperson)

TRC G312

106 Adderley Street, Cape Town, 8001. Tel:(021) 245 161 Fax:(021) 233 285 / 245 225.
Sanlam Centre, 10th Flr, Cnr Von Wielligh & Jeppe Str, Johannesburg, 2001. Tel:(011) 333 6330 Fax:(011) 333 0832/6341.
Metlife Building 9/10th Floor, 391 Smith Street, Durban, 4000 Tel:(031) 307 6767 Fax:(031) 307 6742/49.
[illegible] 5th Floor, 15 [illegible] Street, East London, 5200 Tel:(0431) 43 2885 Fax:(0431) 43 9352/27.
E-mail: [illegible]@global.co.za Internet: http://www.truth.org.za

left and had not taken me with them, and that I had gone as usual to the neighbor's house.

The neighbors, as was common in our village, were an integral part of our family. Our religious beliefs could not be more apart. We were Hindus and they were Muslims, yet apart from us going to our respective places of worship, the family rituals and dynamics were very much alike. We shared our joys and grief, and so they expectantly waited for whatever was going to become the outcome of this encounter.

"What happened?" was the first inquiry. I explained what had transpired and the question raised was, what exactly were the documents about? I confessed that I had no idea, and it was decided that we return to the house and examine it. We entered the lounge and picked up the document that was to change the entire course of my life forever. In bold letters the cover read, "NOTICE IN TERMS OF SUB-SECTION (1) SECTION TEN QUAT OF THE SUPPRESSION OF COMMUNISM ACT, 1950 (ACT NO. 44 OF 1950). Whereas there is in force against you a prohibition under sub-section nine of the Suppression of Communism Act,1950 (Act No.44 of 1950), by way of a notice addressed and delivered or tendered to you, I, PETRUS CORNELIUS PELSER, Minister of Justice, hereby , in terms of sub-section (1) of section ten quat of the said Act, order you for a period commencing on the date on which this notice is delivered or tendered to you and expiring on the 30th day November, 1972, to report to the officer in charge of the Isipingo Police Station, Durban, on every Monday and Friday between the hours of seven in the forenoon and five in the afternoon : provided that this notice shall not apply with reference to public holidays. Given under my hand in Pretoria on this 7th day of December.1967. (Sgd) P.C.Pelser. Minister of Justice." Accompanied with several other restrictions of the above kind in a legal language hardly decipherable at that time, I realized that I had been served with a five-year House Arrest and Banning Orders, which effectively brought my very active political, social, personal and economic life to a sudden end. In a haze, I began to read the restrictions, realizing that nothing was registering in my mind with any intensity. My neighbor, Alladin, on the other hand, who was a much more rigorous and serious scholar, read the document with sustained interest and began explaining the conditions and restrictions that I was to live by for the next five years, and in many cases throughout an entire life. I must admit that I half-heard him, because this came as a shock, although one cannot deny that subconsciously the various scales of punishment for the activities I was engaged in had crossed my mind.

After a while, it was suggested that we leave the documents and retire to my neighbor's house for tea, as was the original plan. Once outside, the bright summer sun shining and the gentle breeze from the Indian Ocean proved comforting for a while as we sat under the China guava tree as usual on the old rattan chairs, drank tea, and chatted about the village matters, although flashes of the Banning Order kept returning to my mind. Dawood and Solly Moosa dropped for the usual chat and were astonished by the turn of events. An hour or so passed when we could hear Kalawathy in the distance shouting to the children to gather their things before the rains brought heavy showers as they normally do in the evenings. On the faraway horizon, one could see the dark clouds, and it was a sure sign that the rains would come pouring down on the village again. Grasscuttia Boywa was heard cajoling his unwilling cows to move on in Ally Road, as he had to place them in the shed before the expected rains. Sheila, who lived many doors away, could be heard collecting her clothes and shouting to the children to bring the clothing basket from the kitchen. Somewhere else, the dogs were barking, for almost every house owned or inherited one of a number of stray dogs, which seemed to coexist with the villagers.

We gathered the chairs and took them to the verandah where they were safe from the rain; saying farewell and thanking the neighbors for the tea, I returned to read the documents. Immediately I realized that by going back to my neighbors, I had violated significant restrictions placed on me. In fact, I had been systematically violating the restriction throughout the afternoon, a situation which years later cost me a trial and a suspended prison sentence of two years.

The storm, which was gathering outside now, struck with fury. Huge raindrops pelted on all sides, and the thunder was accompanied by flashes of lightning which appeared everywhere on the dark night sky. My House Arrest had just begun, both realistically and symbolically in so many ways. At 6 o'clock on that stormy evening my life changed forever.

Chengiah Rogers Ragaven is an International advocate of Human Rights and political freedoms. Banned and placed under House Arrest, Ragaven was later forced into political exile. A revolutionary and an anarchist, he was educated at Oxford, Cambridge, McGill, Sussex, London and Natal Universities. In exile, he worked militantly against racism, militarism, liberalism, sexism and fascist oppression. Among others, he was Head of the African National Congress in Quebec, Canada and a Board Member of International Defense and Aid Fund for South Africa.

He championed, participated, and joined in the struggles of Indigenous People across the World, Feminist Movements and Latin American and African Liberation Struggles. Currently he is working on a book on the Military Regimes and Torture in Latin America (1960-1980). A Fellow of the Simone de Beauvior Institute - a feminist and women's center in Montreal, Canada, he has lectured broadly on human rights and international affairs.

Currently he is a Professor of International Studies in Connecticut, USA.

Lightning Source UK Ltd.
Milton Keynes UK
22 February 2011

167978UK00005B/10/P